DRAMA SKILLS *for* LIFE

L ESLEY C HRISTEN

HEINEMANN • PORTSMOUTH, NH

For my parents

Heinemann
A division of Reed Elsevier Inc.
361 Hanover Street
Portsmouth, NH 03801
Offices and agents throughout the world

This edition is not for sale in Australia, New Zealand, the UK or Europe.
Distributed in Canada by Reed Books Canada, 75 Clegg Road,
Markham, Ontario L6G 1A1

Library of Congress Cataloging-in-Publication Data
Christen, Lesley,
Drama Skills for Life
ISBN 0-435-08636-7
1. Theatre-Juvenile literature. I. Title
792

The Gavemer Foundation wishes to acknowledge the kind permission
of Faber & Faber to print an extract from *Lord of the Flies* by William Golding.

We also wish to thank Houghton Mifflin Company for allowing us to reprint with
permission a section of text from *A Wizard of Earthsea* by Ursula K. Le Guin.
Copyright © 1968 by the Inter-Vivos Trust for the Le Guin children.
All rights reserved.

We acknowledge Octopus Publishing Group Library for kindly granting the right to
reproduce an extract from the text of *The Velveteen Rabbit* by Margery Williams.

First published 1992 by Currency Press, Australia
Production by Gavemer Publishing.
Printed by Kyodo Printing Co. Limited, Singapore
Design, photography and illustration by Jan Thornley
Photographs on pages 128-129 from a videotape by Kirsten O'Loughlin

Acknowledgements

The first and most important influences on my teaching of drama were teachers at the Rusden State College, Victoria. Bronwyn Nicholls' excellent book *Move* was for a long time the 'bible' on which my teaching was based.

In N.S.W. I received invaluable help from the then North Sydney Area drama consultant Lorraine Phelan and Rosemary Lewis, drama lecturer at Ku-ring-gai College.

There have been many other influences for which I am grateful. I would like to mention in particular the inspiration of Peter Brook and Dorothy Heathcote who drew my awareness, in their very different fields, to the importance of myth and legend.

A special thank you to Ian Creighton who patiently helped to edit this text, and to all the students at Korowal School who contributed to the project.

Finally, I would like to acknowledge two people who made this book possible: David Wansbrough, Director of the Gavemer Foundation which funded the book and Jan Thornley whose perseverence and commitment brought the idea of this book to completion.

Contents

Introduction

Drama is very useful both as a specific subject and integrated with other subjects across the curriculum. I believe the real value of drama is to draw out the individual in the child.

The arts are not just ways of providing creative expression. They also provide ways of formulating and giving shape to the students' perception and ideas.

The identification of the arts with creativity and self expression has given them the tincture of remedial education offered to children as an act of compensation for academic work. The arts and drama in particular have been seen as being valuable for the less able child. Drama is, as part of the arts, a particular form of intelligent activity.

Drama, along with the other arts (by which I mean dance, music, painting) are no more important than scientific modes of enquiry but they certainly are as important and as such should be part of any core curriculum.

However, having said this, one would not like to underestimate the creative and expressive importance of the arts, specifically drama. Garry Richardson [founder of Korowal School] in his book *Education for Freedom* emphasises the twofold nature of a complete education. The process of giving out, of expressing a partly realised potential, is seen as a natural balance to the absorption process of learning and can be compared to the way a human being breathes out as well as breathing in. Garry writes:

"It is important to reflect that creativity is not just a matter of art, music or writing poetry. Creativity is involved to a greater or lesser extent in everything we do, in every act of volition."

Creativity can be involved in every subject and every lesson taught in a school. A child sitting motionless in front of a television set is not being creative. The same is true of a class of children sitting in forced motionless silence behind their desks. In his book Garry describes the inter-relatedness of learning and creativity which he says can be considered as polar opposites of the one process:

"The two poles of education find a correspondence in human physiology in the specialised function of the two hemispheres. In most people the left hemisphere

of the brain is the one most concerned with formal learning while the right hemisphere is the one predominantly involved with creative intuitive functions. In addition, there is the corpus callosum, the body connecting both brain hemispheres. It is the task of this body to provide the neural connection which integrate both sides of the brain and both sorts of activities."

One aim of this book is to emphasise the need for creative play within the learning situation. Any teacher of some years classroom experience will recognise that in the absence of consciously manifested creative play all kinds of partially hidden or completely hidden unregulated play will manifest. Hearts being thrown across science labs, notes being sent around the room, scribbling on desks, stirring teachers, are just a few of the less creative versions of such play. Everyone who teaches knows this truth but in most instances it is controlled without recognition of its value as a mechanism of learning and living.

Once I asked a millionaire how he would feel if he lost his money. His reply was that he would perceive such an event as a challenge and that in a short time he would probably accumulate wealth again because the business world excites and interests him. It is a game he enjoys. I suspect that most successful people in business feel the same. They are not frightened of taking risks. How do they get to be like this?

I think everyone has the potential to view the world in the same way. It's just that a lot of us have either had the play squashed in us or it went underground as we seriously undertook combat with the real world.

Drama is a wonderful device for teaching the art of creative play and I consciously use it for this purpose. There is a great deal of difference between creative play and the entertaining teacher. In the former, the class are actively creating; whereas in the latter the teacher as the performer is active while the class is merely reacting. Of course this can lead onto more creative play but more often, I suspect, it ends with the teacher suggesting everyone should now get down to the serious business of work. Someone, somewhere, made this disastrous division between work and play. Of course, the successful teachers like the successful elsewhere know this simply isn't true.

One of the great myths about play is the assumption that when it is happening there will be little concentration and no application. Truly creative play requires enormous discipline and attention. Watch a young group of children playing together and the first thing you notice is the intensity with which they give their attention. This book seeks to promote active and creative learning situations.

Another aim is to demonstrate ways in which drama can extend the knowledge and learning experience of formal study in the discipline of language study.

In this book I will examine how drama can deepen understanding and appreciation of the novel. In this case, *Lord of the Flies* and *A Wizard of Earthsea*. Similarly, the disciplinary skills of formal work will be shown to add depth and quality to the drama lesson.

Traditional education has been subject oriented, each subject being taught as though it were a discrete body of knowledge. More recently, attempts have been made to re-examine this standpoint.

The N.S.W. Education Department has published a document, the k-12 *Language Across the Curriculum*, in which the responsibility for teaching language is now seen as belonging to all subject areas rather than being the sole responsibility of the English faculty. The effect of such a document is to throw open the parameters of specific subjects. As this document tends to emphasise the process as much as assessment of final understandings, it must also raise questions regarding methodology which hopefully will lead to greater exchange between different subject areas as to ways of approaching the process of learning.

It is also important not to confuse the current emphasis on process in the Language Curriculum documents with the notion that content is not important. When one begins to view the curriculum from an integrated approach one is only saying that subjects should be frames of reference.

Although this book will focus on the way in which drama can be integrated into language study, it acknowledges that this is a limitation and sees the need for further development towards an integrated curriculum where teachers of the sciences and social sciences have access to methods which assist a more wholistic view of education.

For example, if a class seven is studying the Celtic people it would also look at Celtic culture. This implies not only looking at Celt geometric patterns but also drawing them in order to feel the shape of the patterns which were psychologically so important to maintain the pattern of life followed. It would also deepen the child's experience to study a novel such as Rosemary Sutcliff's *Song for a Dark Queen* where one witnesses in fiction what happens when such patterns are overthrown; in this case by an invading force.

The reading of Celtic poetry, myth and legend, writing and listening to the Celtic harp would naturally emerge, as would the desire to check with historical evidence and compare the different ways in which language is shaped depending on its purpose. Finally, the magic and mystery of the Celtic religion is a source for new understandings through dramatic expression of the importance of ritual in our lives today.

Drama has the wonderful attribute of being able to offer the chance to widen experience in a very personal way.

Part Three of the book explores the process of the school production. This annual event provides an invaluable learning experience for the students involved. Participation in a venture open to public audience helps to inspire a commitment to excellence.

Indeed, the co-operation between members of a group, while developing a polished performance, is a further benefit of involvement in a school play.

A third aim of this book is to help broaden experience and develop understanding of ourselves and others. This area often referred to as Personal Development is considered so important that elements of it are present in each lesson. It is also the reason that themes whose history extends far back in time are woven into most of the improvisation sections of the work.

These themes in their positive aspect tell about courage, focus, expansion, freedom, acceptance and joy. They are also shown in their negative aspect when we explore fear, greed, limitedness, selfishness, discrimination and domination.

There are many ways of helping students to explore the problems in their lives. I have chosen to avoid psycho-drama and enactment of topical problems and have instead followed a path which explores the above-mentioned themes in a story form similar to the myths, legends and fables of our childhood. Because these forms allow a distancing of emotion it becomes possible to access the humour of the situation and perhaps a better acceptance of our failures.

Stripped of all modern dress and the accompanying emotional overtones, the themes stand out clearly and in my experience allow a more ready acceptance of the issues.

This book acknowledges the importance of the "the hidden curriculum". The best of methods is not sufficient to make a lesson work in terms of students' needs.

Human relationships are the fundamental foundation upon which everything else must be built. When the structures surrounding the teacher support this view, it becomes easier to recognise that moods, attitudes and values expressed by the teacher affect the quality and effectiveness of what takes place.

Lesley Christen

BLACKHEATH, AUSTRALIA

Part One

Lessons

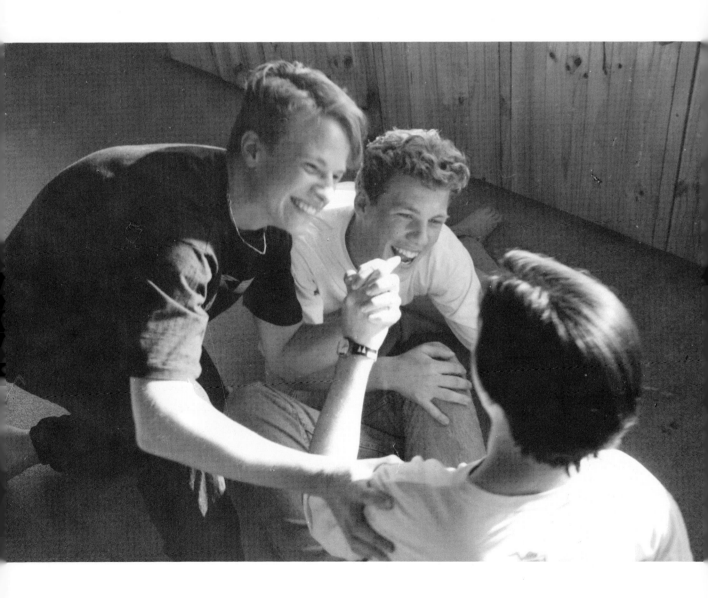

The following lessons assume a progression in terms of the level of difficulty, beginning with simple exercises. By Lesson Fourteen, however, the concepts of concentration, focus and respect on the part of the student would have to be fully understood in order for the lesson to work. This book is a personal view of drama and I have been fairly explicit in each lesson in order to give an insight into exactly how a lesson can develop.

Obviously these lessons are open to individual variation, on the part of both teachers and students. The lesson plans are flexible (however prescribed my description may seem). I have found the time taken for a particular exercise can vary enormously and one exercise can develop in such a way that it takes the entire lesson. This occurs most frequently when I give relaxation and visualisation.

The 'personal development' aspects of each lesson are noted in the italicised marginal comments.

However, because the ideas contained in the exercises are linked, there is a benefit if the lesson can be followed through to its completion.

Lesson time is assumed to be fifty minutes.

Making contact

The Circle

Centering the body:
focus and relaxation

Establishing parameters

Mirroring movement

Lesson One

Centering and Mirroring

Lesson One

After making initial contact with the group it is good to start the first lesson with the exercises listed below. Students often come into the classroom bringing the noise and activity which accompanies a change of lesson. These particular exercises are designed to aid in centering the class. By centering I mean making the students aware of their bodies. Once our attention is focussed on the physical body we calm down mentally. If this doesn't happen, nothing we have to offer will be transmitted. We cannot demand that students concentrate , we can only offer them an experience which will assist this state. In fact, the less we insist on anything and the more we introduce techniques, which bring about change, the more successful we will be and the better we feel about our teaching.

Having said this, however, something should be said about the importance of limits. If anyone has seen the film *Birth of a Nation*, one can witness the "them and us" situation. Most teachers have experienced this at some stage of their teaching career. The answer in the film, as it is in life, is to make "real contact" with the students. But how do we do that in the early stage of acquaintance with a group of students, in a subject which may well be viewed by them to be "mickey mouse"?

If one's attitude towards the work is respectful it creates an atmosphere that what we do has value. In teaching drama, I impose limits and anyone who refuses to respect those limits has to leave. Because drama, unlike so many subjects, touches on the personal, most students will gladly accept those limits.

INITIAL CONTACT

Introducing oneself and sharing interests

At the beginning of the first lesson I always sit with the class. We sit in a circle on the floor and, after everyone has introduced themselves, we begin by finding out from each person what it is they really enjoy doing. Everyone is encouraged to listen carefully to what the other has to say. It is in these early moments that I want to establish my real interest. When those who wish to speak have told about their areas of enjoyment, we sit quietly for a moment absorbing what we have heard. Then I talk about the possibility they each have, to enjoy themselves in the way they have described, without any interference from anyone, in *our* time together.

I want the group to understand that here they have the opportunity to explore themselves, their feelings and to create together. In order to

8

Exercise (a)

Exercise (b)

Exercise (c)

Exercise (d)

Exercise (e)

Exercise (f)

Exercise (g)

Exercise (h)

Exercise (i)

Exercise (j)

Exercise (k)

achieve this, we have to create a special environment in which each one is protected and to assist this there will be limits imposed. We will discuss these after we have done the exercises. An initial contact has been made and now it is time to work physically.

I always play quiet music while we do these exercises. Music by Kitaro or Deuter is suitable but there are other ambient pieces one could use. One has to be prepared to experiment with different types of music in order to discover what is most appropriate.

THE EXERCISES

By doing the exercises with the class and standing in front of them the teacher can be aware of any student having difficulty. It is also extremely important that these exercises are done slowly. This will aid in bringing the student to body awareness. It is interesting to note that the more easily a student can move slowly, the more easily they will relax the body and become focussed.

Stretching exercises

EXERCISES FOR FOCUS AND RELAXATION

a) Feet together, breathe in.
Raise arms above head and stretch whole body upwards so that you are standing on tiptoe.
Slowly breathe out and lower arms.
b) Feet apart, breathe in.
Raise arms to the side.
Hold and stretch.
Lower arms and breathe out.
c) Feet apart, breathe in.
Turn head and body to the left side. The right hand crosses the chest and holds the shoulder. The left arm goes behind the body and rests on the right hip, the palm facing outwards.
Hold position.
Breathe out and turn to the front.
Breathe in.
Turn upper body to the right side, left hand crossing the chest to rest on right shoulder, the right hand behind the back, the back of the hand on the left hip.
Hold position.
Breathe out and turn to the front.
d) Feet apart, stand upright. Hands by side.
Turn body from side to side, letting arms swing loosely following the movement of the body.
e) Body upright. Stretch arms out from the body horizontally. Feet apart, bend knees slowly, towards the floor as you breathe in. Allow arms to sweep towards the floor as though gathering something lying just above the ground. Slowly come up, with the arms crossing in front of the body and sweeping the arms over the head before moving them back to horizontal position. Repeat movement ten times, allowing the movement to become continuous.
f) Lying on the floor, thighs clasped to chest.
Feel the back on the floor. Rotate the back gently so that first one part

Relaxing physically and mentally

of the back, then another, feels the pressure of the body pushed towards the floor. Rotate at least five times.

g) Rock the body with the legs still up so that the thighs are against the chest. Rock side to side and back to front.

h) Squat down. With hands clasping knees, tuck head down. Roll backwards onto shoulders and, without pausing, roll forward. Repeat the sequence ten times. On the tenth movement, the body once again sits poised in the squatting position.

i) Lying on the floor. Bring body up into a V shape, balancing on the bottom. Arms should be stretched out straight.

j) Lying on the floor. Move feet towards the body so that knees are bent. Support ankles with hands. Raise body into bridge position. Hold for the count of ten and then release slowly.

k) Lie on stomach. The hands lie under the thighs to act as support. Lift one leg slowly. Hold in that position for the count of ten. Lower slowly. Repeat with other leg.

Raise both legs together, hold for the count and release.

THE LIMITS   After the exercises we come back to the circle on the floor. I find the floor a comfortable place to sit but this is a personal choice. It does have the advantage however of removing the group from the usual seating structure. This makes it easier for the class to drop those attitudes they associate with more formal seating.

The group is questioned as to what kinds of things they do to gain the attention of their friends when a class is in progress. This can be done in a lighthearted manner. We discuss these methods. They will probably have already employed some of them in this lesson, pushing or nudging each other, catching each other's eye, grinning at each other, making faces etc. We talk about how all of these distract from the central issue which is working by ourselves creatively. It is important that the tone of such discussion is free of judgement. The moment the class feels that the ideas discussed are based on establishing authority rather than respect for the work and oneself they will suspect hypocrisy and miss the point.

THE RULES   I then elucidate the rules which are employed to assist this process.

1. Do not interfere with anyone else's work by distracting overtly. By this I mean nudging, catching someone's eye, laughing to attract attention or making sounds.

2. No talking unless the exercise specifically requires it.

The key signal words are then introduced. These are "freeze" and "relax". The word "freeze" has been abused in the teaching of drama and it is important not to use it as a disciplinary method. I once knew a teacher who would use it as a matter of course at the beginning of each drama lesson to bring the class to order. To do so creates an association in the mind of the class that the word is a basis for control instead of a basis for stillness arising from the need to focus on the students' creativity. For example, students are required to finish any scene they create with a freeze position. This brings the audience to a focal point around the final movement. It helps bring the scene to completion.

The term "relax" is used in relation to the signal "freeze". If the class is doing a series of movements they may be told to freeze in one of the positions. It is good to have one key signal to release the position held so that there is no confusion.

Most of the time we are unaware that we use very little of our power of observation. One exercise to develop focus is to ask a student to perform a simple task. It could be asking them to walk across the room and pick up something before returning to their position in the circle. It is important that no-one in the classroom knows why the task has been set. Another member of the class will be asked to repeat the action exactly as it was done before and the rest of the class to observe its execution. Different students can then offer comment on the accuracy of the repeat performance.

POINT OF FOCUS

This is an extension of the above exercise but here everyone participates. Two students sit opposite each other. One of the students will lead. The other will follow the movement mirror fashion.

The leading students move their arms in time with the music. Three different types of music are used: the first piece is very lyrical and slow. My aim here is to make it easy for the students to follow each other and to sustain the mood of concentration already built up. The second piece can be a little faster to allow the students to play with different moods and the last piece is repetitive in musical form. This is a challenge to them to keep changing the form even though the music is repetitive.

MIRRORING EXERCISE

Working with another person

I use Frank Parsons' *Sounds of Mothership*, J.S. Bach's *Brandenburg Concertos 1-5*, and Vangelis' *Antarctica* in that order.

The Circle

Mime / Movement variations:
light / heavy / tense

Creating a
group sculpture

Lesson Two

Body Awareness

Lesson Two

THE CIRCLE Whhen the class arrives we sit for a short time in a circle. This circle will become increasingly important as we progress through the weeks and the atmosphere encouraged is one of friendship and calm. This time it is good to check that everyone knows each other. When students don't know one another we play a game. This game can begin at any point of the circle. A student gives their name, then the person next to them gives their name plus the person's name who started the game. This continues around the circle so that the last person has to say everyone's name. The game can become more complicated. The group can stand in a circle and a person calls out someone's name and goes quickly to that person's position in the circle. The person whose name has been called has to move away and call some other person's name and go to their space in the circle and so on. This must be done very speedily in order to be fully enjoyed. If everyone in the class is already known to each other the game can take on another form. Each member of the class chooses the name of a plant or flower or animal. Everyone says their name once or twice and then the game as previously described begins.

Once everyone is familiar with each other, we sit down again and go around the circle with each person being asked to say how they are feeling. Some students will be surprised by this question and in the early stages they will all probably say they are okay. My aim here is not so much to elicit information as to let them know that it is good to be aware of how one feels. Sometimes though I will alter my whole lesson plan because of what is said in this exercise. The energy of the group may require something different. But at this stage it is unlikely that they will reveal enough for me to be able to make such a judgement. It is really important to give each student attention, no matter how slight their response. How many times have we been asked how we feel as a matter of course and the person doesn't really listen to the reply?

In the first lesson I establish my parameters. In the second lesson we discuss some of the areas in which we will work.

These areas will include mime and movement, improvisation which may be silent or use voice, games, trust exercises, relaxation and yoga exercises (such as we did in the first lesson). Sometimes we will sit in a circle and exchange experiences. There may be a short discussion about any one of these areas before we move onto the next step of the lesson.

MIME EXERCISES

For this series of exercises a small drum will be used and any instrument which produces a light tinkling sound. I remind the class that there is to be no talking throughout the exercise. I begin to beat the drum and ask the class to feel themselves getting heavier and heavier as they walk around. They are then asked to imagine that they have a heavy load on their back which they cannot remove and to imagine that this load is getting even heavier with every drum beat. It will get so heavy that they can no longer walk upright. I beat the drum more heavily to emphasise this, at the same time telling them that they are now crawling along the ground.

The word "heavy" is repeated often to encourage them to feel that the weight is constantly increasing.

Awareness of different physical experiences

Eventually the weight will be so heavy that they can't move at all. They are trying to move but cannot. I check to see that everyone is really pushing hard against the invisible resistance while still beating the drum very heavily. At the point at which everyone is really involved in the struggle and effort of moving the beats become less heavy. My voice relaxes too as I tell them it is a little less heavy, a little lighter. Now the word "lighter" is said repeatedly and they begin to experience the lifting of the invisible weight.

When they are once again upright an instrument with a light sound will be used, perhaps a triangle, for a short period.

The following exercise is done in silence.

The class is asked to be aware of a feeling of lightness. They stay on the one spot as they transform the feeling of heaviness to one of lightness and I go through the parts of the body using the word "light" after naming each part. They are to keep their eyes closed as the body parts are named and only open them at the end of the exercise.

Then I ask them to move around the classroom very lightly and to see themselves floating like astronauts. They are not to be concerned with anyone other than themselves. (If this kind of work is completely new to the group, it is a good idea not to let them move around the room because it would be too difficult. Instead I would ask them to stay in their immediate space moving only a few steps in either direction.) At this stage recorded music is sometimes used. The best kind of recorded music for this type of exercise is ambient music.

In the final stage I again use an instrument such as the triangle and tell the class that they are to imagine a strange substance keeps emerging from the ground around them. Their object is to move around the room negotiating this substance, expressing the tension experienced. Then they are asked to freeze and experience their body in that position.

Heavy

Light

GROUP WORK   The last exercise of the day is generally shared.
(There will be exceptions to this however.)

The class is put into groups of four (I generally decide on the groups)
and asked to create a still form together. They can choose from any of
the three kinds of experiences we have acted out:

> 1. A feeling of heaviness.
> 2. A feeling of lightness.
> 3. A feeling of tension.

*Experience
of group
co-operation*

Their aim is to create a still form expressing one of these three states in
a group of four people. Because this is their first group work with me the
exercise is a simple one which does not require movement. Some very
interesting sculptural forms can occur.

As light as astronauts

A feeling of tension

Exercises
that introduce elements
of mime

Development of
mirroring movement

Experimenting
with mood changes in
group mime

Lesson Three

Mime / Mirroring / Mood Change

Lesson Three

When the class arrives I ask them to find a spot in the room where they can readily see me and sit down.

We start the lesson with a series of exercises in which we will isolate parts of the body.

These exercises are used to:
1. Develop those body movements and awareness necessary to understand the skills required to mime.
2. Focus the students.

The mime has only the body as a form of expression; it is the only tool available so the user must understand its potential and learn how to control it.

EXERCISES FOR THE HEAD

1. Oscillation. This is a series of "yeses". Watch that the class moves only the head.

2. Side to side motions.
Make a series of "no's".
The movement should be slow. It is important not to push the head too far to the side, otherwise neck strain will result.

3. Side tilts. This is a series of "maybe's".
The head pivots to the side slowly. The tip of the nose should remain pointing to the front.

Before moving onto the next exercise, I talk to the class about the neck and the way it links the head with the rest of the body and ask them what we mean when we call someone stiff-necked.

The class is asked to divide into pairs and sit opposite each other. They are told to sit cross-legged with only a few inches separating their knees. This is important because it encourages co-operation. It gets easier to disconnect with the person opposite the further away you sit.

THE NECK

Understanding emotional body language

1. Each student will take it in turns to hide their neck by pulling their shoulders up and head down.

2. Each student takes it in turn to let their neck grow, become a giraffe—all neck. One feels more graceful and taller.
I tell the class that we send lots of messages with the way we position the neck.

3. Each student is asked to take it in turns to lean back with the neck and then to lean forward aggressively. When we lean back the group will recognise a position of withdrawal.

4. The following forward/backward motions allow the class to experience the mobilisation of the neck. The neck carries the head back and forth. All that should be moving is the neck. The head should be perfectly still and be carried backwards and forewards by the neck.

The class will experience the different parts of the face as instructed. They are still sitting opposite each other and as each part is named they are to move it. I name the following parts:

THE FACE

Forehead, tense and relax.

Nose, twitch from left to right. Screw the nostrils up, relax.

Open the mouth wide and stretch the jaw as far as possible downwards so that the mouth is fully extended.

Smile with the lips closed. Feel the face muscles.

Raise the eyebrows, one at a time if possible and then together, relax.

Pop the eyes forewards and open the eyelids wide. Relax.

It is a good idea to stretch throughout the whole body before moving on to the next exercises. In these exercises it is important that the class remains concentrated.

MIRRORING EXERCISE

Awareness of different emotional states

1. Each student sits opposite another student as before. One student will be the real person and the other will mirror the movements. The real person will imagine they are in front of the mirror washing their face, cleaning their teeth, putting on makeup, shaving, plucking eyebrows etc.

2. The real person and the mirror person exchange roles.

3. Explore the same movements but this time the actions take on, in turn, the qualities of different personalities—angry, joyous, sad, proud, precise, careful.

4. Experiment with mood changes. Real person begins angrily and then becomes happy, or begins carefully but slowly transforms into being sloppy.

Some students will need to be reminded that as this is mime there should be no talking.

GROUP MIME

The class is divided into groups of two or three. A cloak is put in the centre of the room which will be called a 'magic cloak'. When the group comes into contact with the cloak their mood will change and the dynamic will therefore change too. They may be in a celebrative mood for example, on their way to a party when one of them notices this strange object lying on the path. They will tentatively explore this object. It is unlike anything they have ever seen before. One by one they examine it and, as they do, their moods change entirely. This change could be a reaction to a sinister element in the 'magic cloak'. The students will benefit most from this exercise if they move through the stages slowly. The group practises for a few minutes using pieces of material I give them as the magic cloak. Then each group acts out their sequence with the rest of the class as audience. It is important that the rest of the class support each other's effort by being very attentive.

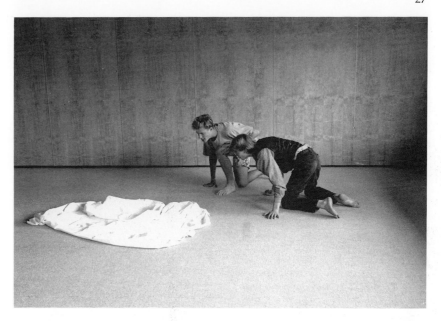

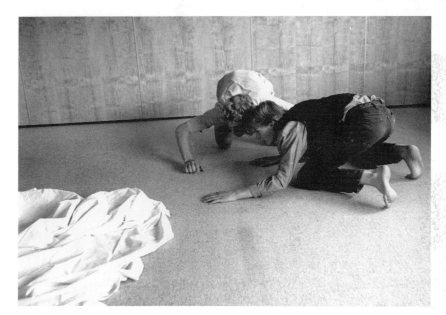

*Movement
and co-ordination
'clown games'*

*Relaxation with
visualisation of a circus*

*'Clowning about'
as mime*

Lesson Four

'Clowning about'

Lesson Four

This lesson will use the principles of mime. All exercises will be done in silence.

Co-ordination

The game we will start with generally evokes laughter which relaxes the class and prepares them for a comic theme. This game begins with me telling the class to run around the room fast without touching anyone. This may be hard for some students and if anyone breaks the rules they are pulled out of the game until the rule is clearly established by the rest of the class. This makes it easier for them to co-operate. On occasions it has been necessary to exclude someone for the entire game. However, it is quite amazing how quickly a class can achieve this exercise.

NUMBER GAME

When everyone has been running for a short time, I call a number. The game requires students to form groups very quickly. The number called indicates how many students can form a group. e.g. If the number three is called, each person will rush to find another two. I give the class ten seconds to form their group and freeze. To begin with, the number called will be calculated in terms of the number of students in the class so that no-one is excluded. If the class size is fifteen the number three or five could be called. We begin with the feeling of what it it like to be included.

Experience of inclusion and exclusion

When a number called excludes a student, this student must leave the game. After each call, the numbers left in the game will reduce, as more students can't find the right amount of partners. The game is completed when only two students remain.

Because students like to run to their friends in this game, I encourage everyone to mix freely by calling each student: A, B or C and stating that each group must contain two of these letters. Between each game number called, the class does different movements. The first movement was running. Movements will be chosen which allow the class to experience different levels as this will become important in the work on clowns which will follow. Other movements could be the following:

1. **Giant steps.**
2. **Hopping.**
3. **Jumping high.**
4. **Sliding around on the bottom.**
5. **Spinning** (they mustn't bump into each other).
6. **Skipping.**
7. **Crow walking.** (This requires the class to squat down and walk around on the balls of their feet.)

8. **Rolling across the floor.** (I don't generally do this until there are only a few left in the game.)

Mime exercises leading up to group improvisation

The class is divided into groups of two. The two then imagine that they are clown tightrope walkers balancing on an imaginary tightrope and walking towards each other. One of them starts to lose balance and the other experiences extreme difficulty in staying on. They wobble and eventually fall off. One then chases the other.

Rules of the chase:

1. No-one touches anyone else or makes physical contact with anyone in the room.

Creative play

2. No sounds. There may be initial excitement in the chase expressed in sound but it is important that the class focus on the dynamic of the chase.

3. Knees up high as they run helps the class to feel like a clown.

4. To introduce facial expression, the class are requested to allow their face to gape as they run.

Relaxation and visualisation

The class is still divided in groups of two. The two clowns are to imagine that they are carrying a bucket of water. One spills the bucket so that the other clown gets wet and the chase begins again.

The class should now be quite breathless, so they are asked to fall on the floor ready for relaxation.

Music from Stravinsky's *Petrouchka* will be used for the visualisation.

Relaxation

The class are asked to do the following:

1. **Make sure the body is in a straight line** with the feet falling gently apart.

2. **Close the eyes and allow the mouth to relax** so that it will be slightly open and the jaw relaxed.

3. **Hands beside the body** but not touching the body, palms uppermost.

The music is kept in the cassette player to be available when needed.

The class is then asked to bring their attention to the parts of the body named. I then proceed through these beginning with the head.

Relax the eyes, the right eye, the left eye, the nose, the right cheek, the left cheek, the right eyebrow, the left eyebrow, right side of the forehead, left side of the forehead, the chin, the jaw, relax. The whole face relaxes. (This will be said very slowly and it is important for me to be conscious of my own state. Am I relaxed? Does my voice have tension in it? If so I consciously relax the parts of the body I name.) After the head, the parts of the body named proceed in the following manner:

Relax the right shoulder	lower arm
the upper arm	wrists
elbow	relax

Relax the palm of the hand, back of hand, thumb, first finger, second, third and little finger. Relax the whole arm.

I then repeat the above as the parts of the left arm are named.

The parts of the back are then named in the following manner:

Right side of the back relax, left side, spine relax, feel the spine become one with the floor beneath. Relax the lower back, the right buttock, the left buttock. Relax the whole back.

Relax the right thigh, right knee, back of the knee, shin, calf muscles relax.

Relax the ankle, the foot, upper foot, lower foot, big toe, 2nd, 3rd, 4th and little toe. Relax the whole foot.

This is now repeated with reference to the *LEFT* leg.

The whole body is then named in the following manner:

Relax the whole body, the whole body quite relaxed, giving in, the whole body relaxed. (If one wished to develop this further, one would go through the parts of the body named and replace the word "relax" with the word "light".)

Visualisation (using music from *Petrouchka*)

I ask the class to picture the following:

There is a big bright blue tent. It is full of people who sit waiting expectantly. Bright lights illuminate the tent. There is the smell of sawdust in the air. I ask them to picture two clowns running into the ring, one clown is fat and slow, the other thin and fast. They trip over each other as they run in. The thin one runs up a ladder and the fat one tries to follow but gets his foot stuck. The thin one pretends to help but ties the fat one's pants to the ladder. The pants tear as he pulls away and he gets angry and chases the thin clown who trips him up. Then the thin one pretends he didn't mean it and they dance together. Just when the fat clown looks happy and relaxed, the thin one dances him into a bucket of water. Now the fat clown is really angry and chases the thin clown who suddenly pretends to be a puppy dog. The fat one pretends to pat him and then gives him a big kick. The thin one now chases the fat clown around the ring and they run under ladders, through a fire ring and their pants catch fire. They run out of the ring.

At the conclusion of the visualisation, the class is brought back to an awareness of the body lying on the floor and asked to breathe in and slowly stretch throughout the whole body, open their eyes and very slowly, sit up.

MIME BASED ON MUSIC   The class is divided into two's and the pairs will develop a mime to the music. In the mime there should be some of the following: climbing, walking on a tightrope, playing tricks on each other, chasing, dancing, pretending to be nice, tripping, showing off. As the class works on developing the mime, the first few minutes of Stravinsky's *Petrouchka* are played over again. Only a few minutes are allowed for the development of the mime and then the groups present them to each other. In the case of a large class this may be difficult. It is important that everyone's work gets shown over a two week period.

'Clowning about'

Visualisation

Playing tricks

Showing off

Chasing

Walking the tightrope

Chasing

Movement and observation
with music

Freezing and
movement on high / medium
and low levels

Brief relaxation

Weaving pathways
to music

Leading and following
in groups

The Circle

Lesson Five

Leading and Following

Lesson Five

The following lesson concentrates on movement as a form of expression.

EXERCISE ONE   I play a game with the class to introduce the ideas we develop later.

One person is to leave the room. The rest of us decide who will begin leading. The person chosen is to decide on the movements and the rest of the class will copy. Everyone follows the movements, but the leader is not identified by position. The class moves in a circular direction around the room. The person outside is invited back in and it is their job to work out who is changing the movement. The movements should be changed every half minute. The movements could include some of the following: walking fast, hopping, swaying from side-to-side, etc.

"I don't always have to lead"

"I don't always have to follow"

It is good to use music which allows fast movement in this exercise. I sometimes use Chris Rea's cassette *Dancing with Strangers*.

Both can be fun

The idea of this exercise is that the group will try hard to disguise who is changing the movement, by focussing closely (but surreptitiously) on the person leading so that there is only a fraction of a second between the leader's new movement and the rest of the class following.

We change the person going out of the room several times.

EXERCISE TWO   The class is requested to freeze in a position and be very conscious of all the parts of the body before they are told to release.

Different parts of the body will create the movement in this exercise. We begin with movements close to the floor (low level). Examples of this: move around the room on bottoms, left hand and feet, knees and arms, and hands, striding, circling, sliding, taking little steps, big steps. The music commences and the class moves, leading with the parts of the body named. [Bright music is used here, e.g. ZZ Top, the Pointer Sisters]

The class will then use different levels:

1. High level. In this level they are asked to allow their movements to stretch high in the air. Appropriate movements would include stretching high, walking on the balls of the feet, giant strides.

2. Medium. This is the level at which we move when we are standing. Appropriate movements, jumping, skipping, hopping, stretching in front.

3. Low. This allows the class to experience movement close to the floor.

Appropriate movements could include moving around on bottoms, knees, one hand and knees, etc.

I then allow them to follow each other in two's. The person leading is free to choose their own movement but they should try to use all the above levels. The pair swap over so that everyone has a chance to lead. The leader of the pair will be requested to change the movement frequently.

Brief relaxation/individual movement

The class lies on the floor.

EXERCISE THREE

I give them a brief relaxation as described in the previous lesson and then play the music of Jean-Michel Jarre, *Oxygen*.

The class are asked to express the feeling of the music with their eyes still closed as they lie on the floor. They are to begin by using their hands only. (As the music is quite 'spacy' in sound, some students may wish to exaggerate to overcome embarrassment. Avoid allowing this to happen at all costs.) They are then asked to move their arms and shoulders, and experiment with moving the torso only. This may be difficult for the more inhibited so I walk around the room encouraging (softly) those who seem more shy. Then they are asked to gradually sit up, with their eyes still closed.

When a new idea is introduced it is good to start by asking very little so that the individual has time to gain confidence. By keeping one's eyes closed the students' concentration is also helped.

As the music becomes faster they are asked to stand up with their eyes closed and move only in a small area around their body. I assist them to get into the feeling of the music by walking around amongst them calling out suggestions: rotate the body, stretch high, stretch low, twist the whole body, shake, rotate the shoulders, the arms.

Students will vary in their response, the shy will probably only make very small movements. They are then asked to open their eyes and to move in pathways around the room.

Pathways

In this exercise the class are to walk quickly, maintaining the rhythm of the music as they walk, not touching but weaving in and out of each other. As the music on the tape gets heavy and slow I ask them to make heavy movements as they form the pathways. (At this point I would switch the tape over.)

EXERCISE FOUR

Pathways: Leading and following

Four people together is a good number for this exercise. One will lead, the others following.

EXERCISE FIVE

I ask them to: a) use all levels

b) use their arms

c) include some rolls

d) include times when they stand on the spot and copy the movements of the stationary leader (mirroring)

Students love to follow each other and this helps the more inhibited.

Each person in the group of four should have a chance to lead the movement. On the tape *Oxygen* there are fast sections and slower sections. The class may be asked to freeze and hold a position for a minute and experience the whole body. While they freeze I will adjust the tape. In this way a variation between fast and slow music can take place. The group can also be asked to break into groups of two or increased to eight.

THE CIRCLE   At the end of this series of exercises, the class moves into a circle. We briefly share feelings and responses associated with the different experiences of the lesson.

Pathways

Pathways

Relaxation

Relaxation

Memory visualisation

Trust exercises

The Circle

Lesson Six

Trust

Lesson Six

For this lesson the students will require pen and paper and/or crayons, coloured pencils, which will be beside them during the relaxation and visualisation. The teacher also needs blindfolds. Make sure there are enough blindfolds for half of the class.

I tell the class that after the visualisation they can either draw or write.

In this lesson we will be experiencing memories of childhood before moving into trust exercises.

We begin with relaxation and visualisation. I ask the class to lie on the floor and repeat the procedures for relaxation outlined in Lesson Four. A relaxation as described in that lesson follows. It is important that no attention-seeking devices (such as coughing, moving) be permitted. If someone has a genuine cough they are quietly told to leave the room, have a drink and only return if they are sure their throat is not going to trouble them.

VISUALISATION   I use the music *Equinox*, by Jean-Michel Jarre. The visualisation proceeds with me talking as follows. It is a good idea to speak very slowly and when an image is suggested, pause to allow the class time to remember and to feel the memory.

"I want you to imagine yourself going back in time to when you were a very small baby lying in a bassinet. Picture yourself lying there, very comfortably. Curl up as if you are a tiny baby feeling very cosy. There is nothing to worry about, everything is taken care of. Feel yourself very warm under the covers. Maybe you have a teddy bear or another favourite toy with you. Picture this cuddly toy. What did it look like? Was it old or new? What colour was it?

Now picture yourself a little older. You are toddling around, possibly dragging something behind you. Try to see yourself. What does it feel like to be you? What are you wearing? Who else is with you? Now let this image go.

Picture yourself a little older, you have started school. Can you remember your first day? What were your feelings? Picture the teacher, the room you were taught in. Now let this image go.

Picture yourself at a birthday, your birthday. Can you see any of your friends? What does your mother, father, or other close relative look like? What games are you playing? See yourself as very happy if that's how you felt. Now let this image go.

You are older now. What is your room like? Do you share it with others? See yourself in your space. What are your feelings? Are you happy or sad? Look around you. What are the things in your room you treasure? Is there anything which you would like to be different? What do you look like? Look in the mirror. See yourself. Are you happy with what you see? Do you feel good about yourself. If you don't, just accept any feelings which arise.

Now come back to the age you are now. See yourself as you are now lying on the floor. Stand behind your head and look down at yourself. Notice how relaxed your body looks. Take a slow, deep breath and very slowly, stretch your arms above your head. When you are ready sit up.

Do not look at or talk to anyone in the class. Choose either the pen and paper or the crayons and either write or draw anything which you remembered strongly from the past."

Self-acceptance

While the class does this, I once again play the music heard while they were lying down. I would allow the class ten minutes for this exercise in drawing.

Self-trust

Either Exercise 1 or 2 below is appropriate at this stage of the lesson.

Like a baby

The class is divided into groups of eight. One person stands in the middle and the rest of the group stand very close together. The person in the middle is moved *gently* around the circle by the group's hands. Before being moved, the person makes sure their body isn't sagging. They hold themselves upright without being rigid. Each member of the group has a turn at being moved *gently* around by the others.

TRUST EXERCISE ONE

**TRUST
EXERCISE
TWO**

Requirement: Blindfolds—these can readily be obtained at a chemist.

The class divides into pairs. One of the students covers his/her eyes with the blindfold; the other student waits and then turns the blindfolded student around (slowly) several times. The blindfolded student is to be taken by the arm gently. It is important to stipulate the word gently. Students through embarrassment in a new situation, can be rough and silly, which defeats the whole purpose of the exercise. The blindfolded student is then led slowly around the room with the sighted student assisting them, exploring a familiar habitat through their other senses. Instructions are given to the sighted student beforehand:

*Trust
of others*

1. Always move slowly unless advised otherwise.
2. Encourage the blindfolded student to touch different textures in the room, the walls, the floor, clothing, objects in the room.
3. Keep any conversation to a minimum. [This is not so much an auditory experience.]

Note: If the teacher has pre-arranged with the students that they bring several harmless substances to taste—food, toothpaste etc.—these can be sited in containers so that the experience can also be utilising the taste sense.

Then, each blindfolded student can be led outside to experience the external environment in a new way. The pairs should all stay within close proximity while the blindfolded student experiences the textures of buildings, soils and trees. If there is an oval or large field, the students can experience running blindfold for a short distance. After ten minutes the pair change over so that both students experience the blindfold situation.

THE CIRCLE

The class finishes in a circle. I encourage the students to comment on any part of their experience.

NaN48

Warm-up exercises

*Developing
focus through repetition
of a simple action*

*Mime
improvisation
emphasising
slyness*

*Group preparation of a scene
incorporating greed
(based on African story)*

*Introducing
gibble-gabble*

*Presentation
of group scenarios*

Lesson Seven

Focus on Action

Lesson Seven

Ａs the students come into the room, they will hear the piece *Winter* from the *Four Seasons* by Vivaldi. I have chosen this music because it is easy to respond to emotionally and I want the class to come into the room experiencing the good feeling most of them would have taken away with them last lesson. Amongst classical music, this particular piece is also likely to be more familiar. Students tend to be receptive to music they don't normally play but have heard before. The music is also a way of developing focus in this lesson. Students entering the room tend to stop talking and become quiet as they listen.

WARM UP   *The Four Seasons* will be played as we do *some* of the exercises described in Lesson One.

All of the following exercises should be performed slowly.

a) Feet apart, breathe in.
Raise arms to the side, hold and stretch, lower arms and breathe out.
b) Feet apart, breathe in, turn body to the left side.
The right hand crosses the chest and holds the shoulder. The left arm goes behind the body and rests on the right hip, the palm facing outwards. Hold position.
Breathe out and turn to the front.
Breathe in.
Turn upper body to the right side, left hand crossing the chest to rest on right shoulder, the right hand being behind the back, the back of the hand on the left hip. Hold position.
Breathe out and turn to the front.
c) Standing upright, hands by side.
Feet apart, turn body from side to side, letting arms swing loosely following the movement of the body.
d) Body upright, stretch arms out horizontally.
Feet apart, bend knees slowly towards the floor as you breathe in.
Allow arms to sweep towards the floor, as though gathering something lying just above the ground. Slowly, come up with the arms crossing in front, before moving them back to horizontal position.
Repeat movement ten times, allowing the movement to become continuous.
e) Lying on the floor, thighs clasped to chest.
Feel the back on the floor. Rotate the back gently, so that first one part,

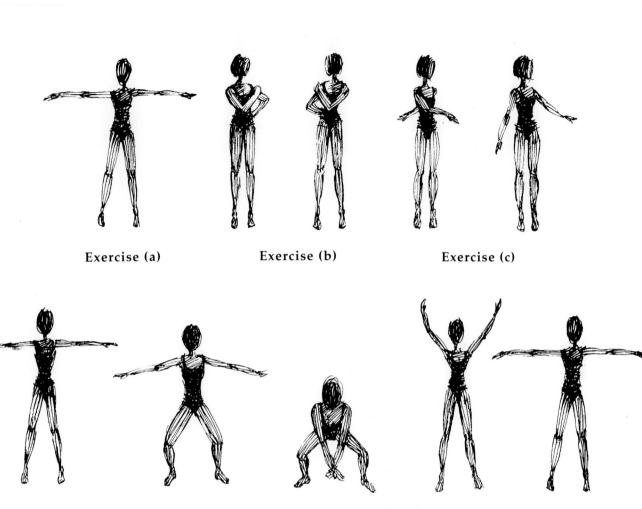

Exercise (a)   Exercise (b)   Exercise (c)

Exercise (d)

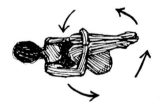

Exercise (e)   Exercise (f)

Exercise (g)

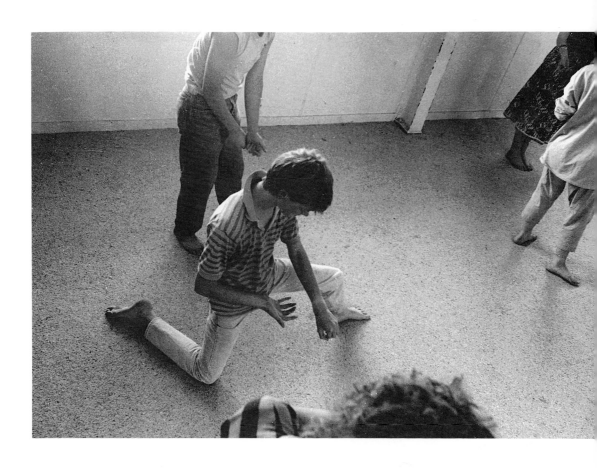

then another part of the back feels the pressure of the body pushed towards the floor. Rotate at least five times.

f) Rock the body after bringing the legs up, so that the thighs are against the chest. Rock side to side and back to front.

g) Squat down. With hands clasping knees, tuck head down. Roll backwards onto shoulders and, without pausing, roll forward. Repeat the sequence ten times. On the tenth movement, the body once again sits poised in the squatting position.

These exercises take about ten minutes. Then I will ask everyone to stand back to back with someone else in the room and rub backs. This will cause some laughter, which of course, is allowed, as long as it doesn't overtake the students for too long. Teenagers can so rapidly move into hysterical laughter.

FOCUS ON ACTION

I replay the piece *Winter* which the students heard as they entered the room. They are then asked to choose an action, a simple action, that is slow and then repeat it several times. Suggestions as to the kind of actions which could be used are as follows:

1. Pouring water into a bucket
2. Picking up a cat and stroking it
3. Putting an arrow in a bow and firing it
4. Serving a ball as in a tennis game
5. Catching a ball which is then dropped and retrieved
6. Brush strokes on a painting

"To give one's attention to even the smallest action is to be fully alive"

The music is used to help the students focus. When they have repeated these actions at least ten times I ask everyone to freeze at whatever point of their action seems to be most interesting. They are then told to relax and sit down wherever they are while each person takes it in turn to demonstrate their action. The aim here is to encourage appreciation of the precision which results when an action is truly focussed. I find there is always at least one student who will demonstrate this. A teacher can rely on the fact that students will witness the focussed action. In drama it is helpful to the students to avoid too much verbal comparison—"Look at how focussed Mary is" etc.

Throwing and catching

THE CIRCLE   In the centre of the circle I place an object. It can be any reasonably light object. I call out someone's name and they quickly go into the centre, take the object and use it in any way other than its true purpose. If it is a chair, it can become a telephone or a television set. Each student has a turn. The exercise must go fast in order to be effective. If a student hesitates, I call on someone else quickly. It is important to insist on speed here so that students move past barriers to creative expression. When we move fast there is no time to reflect on embarrassment, which prevents true improvisation.

GROUP IMPROVISATION

EXERCISE ONE   In preparation for this I ask everyone to stand up and move very quickly to fast music (unfamiliar music so that they are not distracted by fantasy) and, without touching each other, pretend to steal an imaginary object from each other. The object is to relate only momentarily and slyly to each person. We do this for about two minutes.
Music from *Glassworks* by Phillip Glass, piece entitled *Floe*.

EXERCISE TWO   Everyone is asked to freeze and feel the position of each part of their body as they listen. They are to imagine they have in their hand something very important that they want to keep only for themselves; something they don't want to share. They are to think that everyone else in the room knows about it and wants it. They then move around the room expressing this feeling in gesture and other forms of body language, e.g. holding the object close to the body, glancing around slyly, moving stealthily for a few minutes.

The following exercise is done in silence.

EXERCISE THREE   The class divides into groups of two. One of the pair, Person A, is in charge of a fruit barrow in a large town. This person is busy polishing the fruit so it will look good when displayed and takes great care to put all the fruit in order on the barrow. Person B is to attempt to steal one of the pieces of fruit and will need to move cautiously and slyly not to be observed.

Freedom
of
self
expression

Person A has to attend to the fruit and can't stand there just watching Person B. This game has some of the elements of such children's games as "What's the time, Mr. Wolf?" The object of Person B is to take a piece of fruit without being seen.

A variation on this type of exercise is as follows:

Encouraging
self
confidence

The class is divided into groups of three—one of the three could be clumsy, another a show-off and the third the brains behind the group. The three wish to take something from inside a building several storeys high. As they need to break in they may need imaginary ladders, a getaway car, a jemmy, gunpowder (to blow up the safe?).

They mime this event, letting the different characters in the group reveal their personalities. I allow a few minutes for the development of this exercise with the groups working in different sections of the room at the same time. Then we present some of the group's work to each other.

The aim in this exercise is to develop the sense of comedy in the situation, e.g. because of the three personalities. Often the groups don't succeed in their endeavour and are forced into rapid escape.

Using gibble-gabble (sometimes referred to as 'gobbledegook') and gesture I ask everyone to sit down and divide the class into groups of two. Then for one minute we all talk gibble-gabble together as loudly as we like. In ordinary speech, I then tell them that they will act out a scene, using only gibble-gabble, in which one of them has a chicken inside their hut which they don't want the other (a visitor) to know about because they don't want to share it. Of course the other does know about it and is trying to be invited into the hut so that the chicken, once revealed, will have to be shared. They are to be formal and extremely polite with one another and I tell them there must be no pushing or use of physical force to get what they want. They can, however, use cunning such as pretending to be sick etc.

EXERCISE FOUR

They are given two minutes to prepare and may, on request, have a little longer. My aim is to propel them into immediate action where the task is seen to be a challenge rather than a problem to brood upon.

The class present as many scenes as there is time for. With a big class it is impossible to show everyone's work. As my drama classes are never over eighteen in number it is generally possible that most students can show their work and, to enable this, it is reasonable for a teacher of drama to insist on workable class sizes.

PRESENTATION

Focus and
observation

Investigating
modes of dominance:
gesture / movement / verbal improvisation

Circle discussion

Creative play
based on a theme of
dominance

Lesson Eight
Dominance and Submission

Lesson Eight

In this lesson we will bring together some of the skills already introduced to which will be added verbal skills. Verbal skills have not as yet been introduced for the following reasons:

We are by and large a very verbally dominant culture and, students pay little attention to body language and movement in general except when dancing to pop music. In other cultures by contrast rhythm and music dominate. In order to focus on the less dominant aspects of our expression I have found it a good idea to begin a new group by concentrating on mime and movement and to exclude speech. When a class has spent some weeks working in this way introduction of voice seems more appropriate. At first though, as has been seen in the last lesson, by using gibble-gabble, attention is still largely focussed on movement and gesture. In this lesson language is used but the focus of attention is on "not listening" to the content.

We will take the question of dominance and examine it through the following:

> **gesture**
>
> **movement**
>
> **voice**
>
> **improvisation**

The question of dominance is chosen because it is one of the important issues facing teenagers searching to expand their limits.

FOCUS EXERCISE

"Who is carrying the coin?" is the name of the game used. It requires both focus and movement. Someone is chosen from the class to wait outside. Before this student returns to the room, one of the other students is asked to initiate a movement which the rest of the class will mirror as they move around the room to music. Sometimes, I call out the different types of movement. The movement must be changed every thirty seconds. Another student holds the coin and must attempt to pass it without this action being seen by the person who was sent outside. Once the student returns to the room, the game commences. The game requires that the coin be constantly moving from one person to another. Each person has also to concentrate on the movement which is constantly being changed. After a couple of minutes has passed I ask the person who stood outside to guess who is holding the coin. We may repeat this several times and allow a different person to wait outside.

The class is divided into pairs. One of the two will gesticulate an action, using head arms and legs (where necessary) which the partner is to perform. There must be no verbal assistance. Then the pair swap over so that the one who formally gave the directions, now enacts them.

I make suggestions as to the kind of action which could be used:

running on the spot / touching the toes / jumping up and down

GESTURE

1. The pairs are asked to sit down quietly opposite each other with their legs crossed so that the knees are only a few inches away from each other. It is important for this exercise that the pair are close. They begin talking at the same time as each other after I give them the subject "What I did when I got up this morning". It is important to insist that there be no shouting to achieve dominance. The object of this exercise is to be so interesting that the partner will want to stop and listen. Once this is achieved the pair should stop and put their hands in the air. The groups are changed around when this happens and those who proved to be the more dominant are put into pairs while the less dominant work with each other.

2. One person from the class is designated to sit on a chair at the front. This person is invested with authority, e.g. head teacher, boss, policeman etc. We decide what the person's authority is and then line up and individually approach them with a greeting of some kind. The greeting will be improvised. This exercise gives an awareness of the different voices we employ when approaching a situation where we feel dominated. The impact of the exercise can be best felt if the class moves quickly, one by one, and take several turns at improvising in this situation.

VERBAL DOMINANCE

1. The class stands up. They are to move quickly in straight lines. They change direction only when they hear the beat of the drum. When they come to a wall or obstacle they must mark time until they hear the drum beat which permits them to change direction.

We do this for a few minutes so that they have the experience of what it is like to move *only* in straight lines.

2. I ask two or three students (depending on the class size) to stand at the end of the room in a straight line and the rest of the class to advance slowly, also in a straight line, from the other end of the room towards them.

DOMINATION THROUGH MOVEMENT

We form a circle and I ask everyone, particularly the group of three, to say how they felt. We discuss the feelings which have arisen that day throughout the various exercises. I don't encourage the students to talk about how these experiences translate into other experiences at home or at school. Instead, we focus on feelings which arise within the given situation. While psycho-drama has a place in the work of the drama teacher, the focus can too often, with teenagers, become a "them and us" (teachers versus pupils, parents versus children) situation where the students see themselves as victims. It seems wise to encourage within

THE CIRCLE

the students the feeling that they are personally responsible for their actions and feelings and that they need not be victims. People around them are generally doing the best they can, given the circumstances in which they find themselves. Most situations have a solution if we look carefully enough.

Exploration of dominance and submission

The subject that we have taken for the day is:
a) What it feels like to be in a situation where someone is dominant.
b) To be able to express what that feels like.
c) To experience what it feels like to be dominant.
d) To play with this situation creatively to take away some of the heavy emotion invested in it.

In taking this approach the aim is not to find solutions for students but to increase their creative power when they feel blocked so that it may be possible for a creative solution to be found.

I divide the class into two's and ask them to sit opposite each other. They are to imagine that they are both in a hurry. They are each in a car and both need the one remaining parking space in the hospital car park. Each person has an excellent reason for taking the one remaining space. Each should try and convince the other why they should have the space.

CREATIVE PLAY WITHIN A SITUATION OF DOMINANCE

The emphasis is to be on communication rather than confrontation.

They work on this for a few minutes and then I call for silence and ask them if anyone found a solution. In the time remaining we discuss what happened.

Domination through movement

Tunnel game

Brief relaxation

Visualisation:
Struggle and freedom

Drawing
on the subject of freedom

Preparation and presentation
of mime on this theme

Lesson Nine

Struggle and Freedom

Lesson Nine

TUNNEL GAME

When the class comes into the room they see that the chairs and desks have been set up in such a way that they form a long tunnel. The tunnel is narrow and there are chairs at odd angles making it difficult to pass through without touching. At various points the tunnel is broken and a chair on its side provides an obstacle which must be crossed. I tell the class they have only one chance to negotiate the tunnel without touching the sides. If any article of clothing touches the sides an alarm (a whistle) would be sounded by me and they are caught. Each student in turn passes through the tunnel. The students help me dismantle the tunnel and then I ask them to prepare for relaxation.

**RELAXATION
AND
VISUALISATION**

Each student lies on the floor. Beside each student I place a large sheet of white paper and some coloured crayons.

I give the students a short relaxation as described in Lesson Four. At the end of this relaxation the music by Vangelis from *Antarctica* is played. As the music plays I describe the following situation:

"Imagine you are all husky dogs and you have been accidentally left tied up by humans who have had to leave in a hurry. Feel the restriction of the rope. How are you tied up? Is it by the legs or around the neck? Feel the part of the body which is restricted. Now begin to move those parts of the body which don't feel restricted. Enjoy the freedom of the movement. Now come back to that part which feels constricted. Try to move it, feel a sense of struggle. You don't like feeling tied up. Look around you at all the others also constricted. Notice their bodies. Don't look at their eyes, just witness their struggle. No sounds. Come back to your own body. Now I want you to really begin to struggle, to want to get free. Feel the desire for freedom sweep throughout your whole body. It can be done if you try hard enough and give it your full concentration. Those of you who really want to try hard enough will become free."

*Exploration
of constraint,
struggle
and freedom*

I am silent and allow the class to experience this struggle. They are told they can relax quietly on the floor and when they are ready to slowly sit up and, without looking at anyone else, draw any picture they want on the subject of freedom.

I allow them ten minutes to do this and then ask them to move into groups of two and share the ideas behind their drawings with each other. The music continues softly.

Each group is asked to prepare a mime in four minutes on the theme of freedom. As many of these as can be presented in the time remaining are shown to the whole group.

MIME IMPROVISATION

Chasing game

Inner strength exercise:
confronting challenge

An American Indian story:
'Jumping Mouse'

Mime embodiment
of inner strength

The Circle

Lesson Ten
Confrontation and Inner Strength

Lesson Ten

Oˣne of the attractions which ski-ing has for me is the challenge it presents. One is faced with the fear of speed, the fear of falling over and hurting oneself. It is the challenge of mastering movements which don't come naturally and its delight is the mastery of all these.

We can also use drama to challenge our fears just as little children do when they play chasings or "Murder in the Dark" or "What's the time Mr. Wolf?" In this lesson the class will play with the concept of confrontation.

EXERCISE ONE

One third of the class spreads themselves out in different areas of the room and become as statues. The rest of the class pairs off; one of the pair will be the chaser, the other will be chased. They are not to touch another person in the room as they run. I give the signal to begin by clapping my hands. This activity is to be done without talking or loud noise. It is important to insist on this. If you watch little children playing "What's the time Mr. Wolf?" they will be totally concentrated as they move forward and it is this quality which is the object of the exercise. The students may show some physical expression of excitement in what we call "body language". After a short time the students change around so that everyone has a turn. The ratio of those being statues remains the same.

EXERCISE TWO

The class is divided into groups of four. Two students—students 'A' and 'B' sit opposite each other. Student 'A' will mirror the movements of student 'B'.

The two other students: 'C' and 'D' will be standing (or sitting) on either side of the first two students 'A' and 'B'. Student 'C' will ask an easy arithmetic question. Student 'D' will ask about events in student 'A's' life. They will ask these questions alternatively and continuously.

Thus student 'A' has to:

Using focussed attention to confront a challenging situation

1) **mirror student 'B'**
2) **answer questions from student 'C'**
3) **answer questions from student 'D'**

Everyone in the group of four will rotate roles after a few minutes so that all have a chance to be in the "hot seat".

Everyone finds a place on the floor a little away from the rest of the group. I tell them to close their eyes and imagine that they are a tiny mouse curled up. They are to move around their small space as if they were a mouse, doing mouse-like-things; collecting, investigating, examining, sniffing (quietly), building a nest. This is to be done with eyes closed and as noiselessly as possible. Then I ask them to be very still and to lie down quietly to listen to a story I know by heart. In drama I never read a story because I believe I tell a story quite differently when I really know it.

This story is from American Indian medicine legend. *Jumping Mouse* illuminates the importance of personal courage. It shows how one can confront one's fears and grow as a human being. It tells of how the mouse is transformed into an eagle. This story is presented below. Of course, other stories of personal courage may be used instead.

The Story of Jumping Mouse

Once there was a mouse. He was a busy mouse, searching everywhere, touching his whiskers to the grass. He was very busy doing mice-like things. But once in a while he would hear an odd sound, which would make him lift his head and he would wonder. One day he scurried up to a fellow mouse and asked him, "Do you hear a roaring in your ears, my brother?".

"No, no", answered the other mouse, not lifting his busy nose from the ground. "I hear nothing. I am too busy now. Talk to me later."

The little Mouse shrugged his whiskers and busied himself again. But there it was, that faint roaring again. One day he decided to investigate the sound and scampered a little way off from the other busy mice. He was listening hard when suddenly someone said "hello".

"Hello, little brother", the voice said. The mouse looked in the direction of the voice. "Hello", again said the voice. "It is I, Brother Raccoon. What are you doing here?"

"Just investigating", said the little Mouse timidly. "I hear a roaring in my ears."

"A roaring in your ears?" replied the raccoon, "What you hear, little brother, is the river."

"The river?" the mouse asked curiously, "What river?"

"Walk with me and I will show you the river", Raccoon said.

Little Mouse was terribly afraid but he was determined to find out about the roaring and so he told Raccoon he would go with him to the river. As he walked along his little heart pounded. Raccoon was taking him along very strange paths. Finally they came to the river which was huge and breathtaking.

"It is powerful!" little Mouse said.

"It is a great thing" said Raccoon. "Let me introduce you to a friend and then I must go."

"Welcome, little brother", said a large green frog sitting on a lily pad, "Welcome to the river. Would you like some magic medicine power?"

Little Mouse looked at the river and saw all the little pieces of the world carried along on its surface.

"Medicine power? Me?" asked little Mouse.

"Yes, yes, if it is possible," was the reply. "Crouch as low as you can and then jump as high as you are able!" Frog said.

Little Mouse did as he was instructed. He crouched as low as he could

*Exploring
personal strength
through
risk-taking*

and jumped. And when he did, his eyes saw the sacred mountains. He could hardly believe his eyes. But there they were, the sacred mountains! Then he fell back to earth, falling into the river and getting very wet. He was frightened nearly to death.

"You have tricked me" little Mouse screamed at the Frog.

"Wait", said the Frog, "you are not harmed. Do not let your fear and anger blind you. What did you see?"

"I" stammered little Mouse, "I saw the sacred mountains."

"And you have a new name", said Frog, "It is Jumping Mouse."

Jumping Mouse was so excited at what he had seen that after thanking frog with all his heart, he hurried straight back to the world of mice.

But no-one would listen to his story. And, because he was wet and had no way of explaining it because there had been no rain, the other mice believed he had been spat out of the mouth of another animal who had tried to eat him and if that was the case he must be poisonous altogether.

Jumping Mouse tried to live once again with his own people but it was impossible.

The memory of what he had seen was too strong. It burned in his mind and heart and so he decided to journey to the sacred mountains.

He went to the edge of the land of mice and looked out onto the prairie. He looked up into the sky and saw it full of many black spots, each one was an eagle. And he felt very afraid.

But he was determined to go to the sacred mountains and so he gathered all of his strength, took a very deep breath and with his heart pounding fiercely, he ran right out into the prairie. He ran until he reached some sage bushes and there he rested and tried to catch his breath when he saw an old mouse. The old mouse was very busy collecting and gathering things.

"Hello" said the old mouse, "welcome".

Jumping Mouse said, "This is truly a wonderful place and the black spots can't see you. Can you see the sacred mountain?"

"Yes and no", said the old mouse, "I know of them but I can't see them. It is too dangerous to go further across the prairie. Stay here with me and you will be very comfortable, gathering and collecting."

"Thank you very much", said Jumping Mouse, "but I must seek the mountains."

"You are very foolish", said the old mouse.

It was hard for Jumping Mouse to leave but he gathered his determination and ran hard again. He could feel the shadows of the spots on his back as he ran. Finally he ran into a stand of chokecherries. It was cool there and very spacious. There was water, cherries, seeds to eat, grasses to gather for nests, holes to explore, and many other busy things to do.

He was busy investigating when he heard a very strange sound. It came from a mound of fur with black horns. It was a great buffalo.

"Such a magnificent being" thought Jumping Mouse and he crept closer.

"Hello, my brother", said the buffalo.

"Hello, Great Being", said Jumping Mouse, "Why are you lying here?"

"I am sick and dying", the buffalo said, "and my medicine has told me that the only way I can be cured is to obtain the eye of a mouse. But I don't even know what a mouse is".

Jumping Mouse was shocked and quickly ran back to the other side of the chokecherry bush. He listened to the terrible rasping breath of the dying buffalo and, although at first he felt relieved that the buffalo didn't know he was a mouse, he also began to feel very sad that such a great beautiful being would soon die.

He went back to where the buffalo lay and said in a shaky breath, "I am a mouse. I cannot let you die, you are so great. I will give you one of my eyes." And with that, one of his eyes flew immediately out of his head and the buffalo was made well.

The buffalo jumped to his feet and said, "Thank you, little brother. I know of your quest for the sacred mountains. Run under my belly and I will take you right to the foot of the sacred mountains and you will be safe from the black spots".

Little Mouse ran under the buffalo, secure and hidden from the black spots but with only one eye it was frightening. Finally, they came to a place and buffalo stopped.

"This is where I must leave you, little brother", said the buffalo.

Jumping Mouse felt a little nervous being left with only one eye but he thanked the buffalo and immediately began investigating his new surroundings.

Suddenly he came upon a grey wolf who was sitting there doing absolutely nothing.

"Hello, brother wolf", Jumping Mouse said.

The wolf suddenly sat up, his ears alert and cried, "Yes, yes, That's what I am. I am a wolf." But then, very soon, his eyes dimmed and he sat quietly without any memory at all.

"Such a great being", thought Jumping Mouse, "but he has no memory."

"Brother wolf", Jumping Mouse said.

"Wolf, wolf", said the wolf.

"Please, brother wolf, I know what will heal you. It is one of my eyes. Please take it."

When Jumping Mouse stopped speaking his eye flew out of his head and the wolf was made whole.

"You are a great brother", said the wolf. "But now you are blind. I am the guide into the sacred mountains. I will take you there."

The wolf guided the mouse through the pines, up the huge sacred mountains to the medicine lake at the very top and, because Jumping Mouse couldn't see, he told him of all the wonderful sights from the top.

"I must leave you here", said the wolf, "but others will guide you."

"Thank you", said Jumping Mouse. But when the wolf was gone Jumping Mouse felt very alone and frightened.

He felt a shadow on his back and heard the sound that eagles make. He braced himself for the shock. And the eagle hit.

Jumping Mouse went to sleep.

Then he woke up. The surprise of being alive was great. Now he could see but everything was very blurred.

"I can see! I can see!" said Jumping Mouse over again and again.

A blurry shape came towards Jumping Mouse who squinted hard but couldn't make it out.

"Hello, brother", a voice said, "Do you want some medicine?"

"Yes, yes", said Jumping Mouse.

"Then crouch down as low as you can and jump as high as you can" said the voice.

Jumping Mouse did as he was told. The wind caught him and carried him high in the sky.

"Do not be afraid" said the voice, "Hold on to the wind and trust".

Jumping Mouse did. He hung on to the wind and it carried him higher and higher. Jumping Mouse opened his eyes and he could see clearly. Everything was clear and bright.

"Now you have a new name", called the voice, "You are Eagle."

EXERCISE FOUR   *This should take about 3-4 minutes*

At the end of the story the class is asked to stretch without opening their eyes. I play the first few minutes of *Harmonic Ascendent* by Robert Schröder (any inspirational music would serve equally), and ask the class to rise from being the tiny mouse to a strong figure in whatever shape that happens. They are to move very slowly at first and not to rush, to allow the feeling of strength to develop slowly and purposely. When everyone is standing, they are asked to feel the power throughout the whole body.

Growing in strength

Feeling the power

We finish the lesson in a circle. The time allowed for personal expression of feelings, completes the experience. Some students will not want to say anything and that is fine. They gain a lot from listening to others who find it easier to express their feelings.

THE CIRCLE

Modified
Martial arts exercises

Group work
using concepts of stability,
disturbance and resolution
(based on theme of Japanese film)

Introducing
sound and speech

Lesson Eleven

Stability / Disturbance / Resolution

Lesson Eleven

A

As has already been suggested we are a very verbal culture in which children are heavily exposed to audio-visual communication through television. There is, therefore, a strong chance that they will readily surrender their unique view of the world to the greater wisdom of their favourite television programme. By delaying the use of verbal communication they have a chance to develop a more creative approach to mime and movement. Therefore verbal communication is almost excluded from the course until Lesson Eleven.

Television scenarios are avoided. Myth and legend are used to assist this creative aim. The legend or story may be relatively modern, as in the case of *The Seven Samurai*, a film whose script will help to create the basic story line of this drama lesson.

EXERCISE ONE   The exercises which follow are found in the martial art called Tae Kwon Do. (Before teaching these exercises, knowledge of martial art is recommended).

Tae Kwon Do
Group is in lines with good separation between each line.

Exercise A—Warm up
1. Place feet shoulder width apart, parallel to each other.
2. Bend knees, keeping trunk upright to give body a coiled spring action.
3. Clench fists tightly.
4. Bring right arm back close to body so fist is facing upwards and close to chest.
5. Extend left arm fully forwards with fist facing downwards.
6. Punch with right arm extending forwards while returning left arm to the left side of the body. The fists change from the upward to downward position while this action is executed.
7. Added power to the punch is gained from the turning motion of the fist while the arm is extending and exhaling forcibly during its execution.
8. Variation on this warm up:
a) Before right arm punch, right foot describes a circle behind left foot and body twists to the right 90°.
b) Right foot extends 90° to left foot as right hand punch is executed.

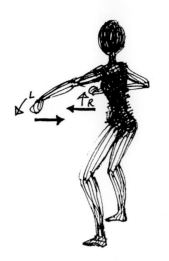

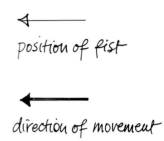

position of fist

direction of movement

Exercise (a)

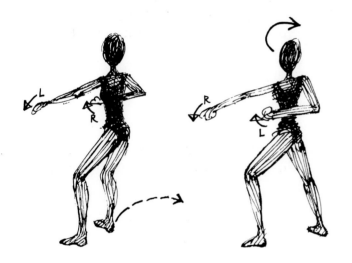

Variation on (a)

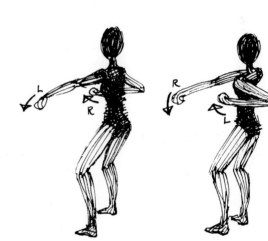

90° turn to right

Exercise (b)

c) A left and right hand punch is executed in quick succession and the manoeuvre is repeated, thus turning a full circle in 90° sections.

Exercise B
1. While running in a circle a jump is made springing from the left leg.
2. The right knee is brought up high to the chest.
3. At the apex of the jump the left leg is extended into a kick, gaining more force and height from the extension of the right leg downwards.
4. The increase in the height of the kick in this exercise is to concentrate maximum force. A normal kick would have lost a lot of its force by the time it reached head height.

EXERCISE TWO   The students are told that the following actions must be performed silently. The class sit down in a group. I call a student to me and quietly tell him/her to imagine that they are drawing water from a well and taking it to a field where they are to water some young plants. The student is asked to be very concentrated in the action so that the rest of the group are very clear what the action is about. The rest of the class watches. When this student has shown some of the action, another student is called aside by me and asked to start lighting a fire.

Gradually the rest of the group is involved in the following actions:

> **collecting wood**
> **building a hut**

In this activity four people are introduced one at a time. The first one will be adding water to mud, the second will be shaping the mud into a square shape, the third will carry the brick to the site and help the fourth to construct the hut. Some others will:

> **be planting a crop**
> **be washing clothes in a river**

The rest, with the exception of three students, will cook in individual huts, make hunting and planting implements, or weave.

Developing
personal strength
through
confronting
fear

When everyone has been performing these actions for a few minutes, all are asked to relax but remain still while they are given a brief outline of what is going to happen. "In a short time there will be a disturbance of some kind and you must all react from a position of fear." I remind them of the mouse they portrayed the week before and tell them that when the disturbance occurs they are to react as if they were the mouse and then to continue with their previous activity. After the disturbance has occurred, they are to hold a village meeting about what can be done.

The students left out of the action will be students who find it easy to be strong and powerful. They will provide the disturbance. They are taken aside while the following is explained. They are asked to imagine they are riding into the village on three large horses. They are to make a lot of noise and sound very fierce. When they have ridden into the village they will tell the villagers in a strong manner that they are taking over the village well and they will take away anyone who tries to prevent them. They are then to gallop away after threatening to return the next morning. The villagers hold their meeting.

I let the action unfold and observe the process. If the group appears stuck, I may suggest the following resolution:

"Become fierce and make a lot of noise to frighten away the intruders the next morning."

I may also follow up this lesson by showing the students the film *The Seven Samurai* by Japanese director Kurosawa.

The 'disturbance'

The 'bully'

The 'fear'

The village meets

Group strength

Focussed listening

Preparation exercise:
Rhythmic
swirling and turning

Improvisation
of sound patterns
and
complimentary
movements

Creative play
on a theme of ritualistic
movements

The Circle

Lesson Twelve

The importance of Ritual

Lesson Twelve

Whe the class enters the room each person is offered a blindfold. This is in preparation for the first exercise. In Exercise Five of this lesson, earth-coloured face paint will be used.

EXERCISE ONE   The class is divided into pairs and each pair is to secretly devise a sound. The pairs are then split and led by me to different parts of the room. Each group of two must try to discover each other through sound. I select four saboteurs, telling them quietly to remove their blindfolds. The rest of the class will remain ignorant of their presence. The saboteurs are to try to prevent the meeting of the pairs by imitating their sound and leading them astray.

This exercise requires skill in listening if one isn't going to be foxed. Once a partner is accepted they are to put both hands in the air. I can of course only do this once without the class knowing about the saboteurs. Once they find their 'partner' they have only ten seconds to be certain and then they must put up their hands. This exercise can also be used without saboteurs.

EXERCISE TWO   The class is asked to lie blindfolded on the floor and when they are lying quietly, I move across the room in a sequence of movements; for example, shuffling, heavy dragging, skipping, swirling. The group are then asked to tell me the sequence of movements.

I do another sequence of movements and ask the question once more. The teacher could substitute sound for movement. Students then raise their bodies to indicate direction of sound. (Instruments could be used.)

EXERCISE THREE   Music by Irene Pappas and Vangelis is used in this section. For many students it is unusual music, with ritualistic sound patterns and at first its strange drama may evoke amusing movements. This can be allowed. Play at this stage is important. We have by now established mutual trust. This music is used because it introduces chanting patterns which will be taken up in the next exercise. After a couple of minutes of play we all stand in a circle and each person takes it in turn to put on a blindfold and experience slow turning within the circle. Sometimes two turn at once if I judge there is no likelihood of collision. I generally allow them to go around the inside of the circle twice. Participating in movement in this way is a kind of ritual and allows the class to be more open to the next

Unself-conscious expression within a group

exercise which, for many, will require letting go of the fear of exposure since they will be moving by themselves to the the chant of the group.

EXERCISE FOUR

We sit in a circle and I begin beating a simple rhythm on my knees. The class is asked to follow the rhythm, beating the pattern on their knees. When this has been established, a sound phrase is added which they echo. After we have experienced the sound pattern for a minute or so another member of the group is asked (by use of gesture) to take over and everyone has a turn in leading the group. I speak now for the first time in this exercise in order to tell the class the next step. I will lead with a sound pattern and everyone will take it in turns to go into the centre to perform a movement. They need only be there for a few seconds. At this stage we often take it in turns to make silly sounds and this always seems to bring the class back easily from the experience of being a little exposed on an individual level.

*Group
co-creation*

EXERCISE FIVE

The class divides into pairs. We paint our faces with face paint. This will take only a few minutes. Each pair decides on a fixed sound pattern,
      eg., "He hee, hi ho hum;
         Hento Marko,
      Fe, fi fum!"
One person will lead, the other will follow the leader's movements as they chant. They are encouraged to develop new movements.

They then swap over positions, decide on a new chant and again, one will follow as the leader tries out new movements.

THE CIRCLE

We finish the Lesson with a brief circle where we exchange experiences.

The Circle

*Recollections
of witch and wizard
stories*

*Embodiment
of a witch or wizard*

*Improvisation
on the weaving of
a spell*

*Describing
the spell in gibble-gabble*

*Improvisation
on the theme of innocence
and evil*

Lesson Thirteen

Playing with Power

Lesson Thirteen

*Experiencing
a sense
of personal
power*

Whhen the class comes into the room they will notice various articles lying around the room. One might be a witch's hat or a broom or a black cloak. We form a circle.

THE CIRCLE   Once in the circle we try to remember any stories from childhood to do with witches and wizards. I always remember so vividly the moment in *The Wizard of Oz* when the face of Dorothy's aunt became the witch's face and so I start by sharing that scary moment. The group relates similar memories before we move onto the next exercise.

EXERCISE ONE   The class is asked to separate out and each person to find a space of their own. Everyone is to take on a shape which best represents their idea of a witch/wizard. They can choose to be a dark or a strong and beautiful power. They are asked to imagine they are very powerful and that they are making a very powerful spell. They are to imagine a cauldron in front of them into which they are putting strange mixtures. I suggest they sing a special chant to complete the spell.

EXERCISE TWO   Music by Sehnsucht, called *Finklang* is played. The first few minutes of this piece are played. Any strange music evocative of witches and wizards is suitable. A teacher with musical skills will be able to create their own music to evoke this atmosphere. The class is asked to use weaving movements in the air where they are standing. They are to imagine they are weaving a spell in the air. They are required to use all levels—high, medium and low—as they spread the spell further out from themselves and eventually to involve someone near them in the weaving process. I ask them to use stillness as well as movement in their weaving.

EXERCISE THREE   Each person in the class is to sit opposite the person with whom they were weaving the spell. They are going to tell the person opposite in gibble-gabble about the spell they have just woven, what its purpose is and what they were mixing.

IMPROVISATION   In this improvisation my aim is to elicit something of the experience of Commedia del' Arte. Working in the same pairs the class are to imagine that one of them is very evil and plotting to give the other one poison. The other person is a friendly innocent who never realises the mischief of the other. The feeling quality of this improvisation is to be humorous rather than serious. The nasty one is to let the audience know, through actions and gibble-gabble, that mischief is afoot. All the signs will be there for the innocent one to read the intention of the nasty one but, because he/she is innocent, they never guess. The pair will decide the outcome, i.e whether the innocent one will become sick or whether the nasty one gets caught in his/her own trap or whether they both escape.

Frequently, I will extend this theme so that each group is larger and we include other characters such as a mischievous cat and a cunning magician's assistant. By this stage, the group will enjoy the experience of sharing their work with a wider audience. Arrangements are made for other classes to provide an audience for the work they are doing with each other. This kind of improvisation is very popular with younger classes and in my school, which is both primary and secondary, we always take some of our work to the younger classes who love the fairy tale quality.

Weaving a spell

Magic in the cauldron

*Sculpting
a deformed person*

*Experiencing
being a deformed person
in the presence of
an audience*

*Experiencing
rejection*

*Surmounting
rejection with creativity*

*The Circle:
sharing / drawing
writing*

Lessons Fourteen and Fifteen

Experiencing being Different

Lesson Fourteen

We talk a lot about overcoming prejudices towards people who are different but unless we become the subject of this prejudice and feel what it is like to be isolated, examination of such issues is an academic exercise. Recently, I witnessed a performance by Sue Ingleton in which she enacted the role of an old woman of our culture. She played this role with such poignancy and humour that I was enticed into the experience of what it might be like for me when I am old.

She was also putting me in touch with a similar issue to that raised in the entry *Public Face, Private Eye* in the 1988 Australian Video Festival, which, examines the invisible people of our culture, in particular the inmates of a mental hospital. The Bouffon tradition of acting allows the individual to get closer to this experience because we have the opportunity to be in the shoes of the outsider, the rejected. Before embarking on this experience, it is important that the group has reached a certain level of maturity. I don't mean however maturity in years, but rather maturity in terms of the quality of relating within the group and each teacher has to assess this for themselves.

The students need to be told at least a day in advance to wear very loose-fitting clothing for this lesson. If it is possible I arrange with other members of staff to do the following two lessons together over one hundred minutes rather than fifty.

Props needed for the two Lessons (fourteen and fifteen):
   a pole for the teacher
   pillows
   cotton wool balls
   different lengths of material
   8 tennis balls
   different extracts from Shakespeare or other pieces of literature
      —depending on the level of students.
Pieces I use are Gloucester's speech from *Act I Scene 1 of Richard III* and the ghost's speech *Act I Scene 5 lines 9-23 of Hamlet.*

Poems from any of the following:
   e.e. cummings
   Emily Dickinson
   G.M. Hopkins
   Kath Walker   [as well as nursery rhymes, songs]
When the class enters the room I ask those who feel like taking a risk to raise their hands. It works best if about half of the class form this

group.The group who identified themselves as risk-takers are to find a space separate from the others and the other half are asked to go and collect material and a pillow. They take these materials and stand in front of someone they haven't worked with recently. When this is done, the whole group is asked to sit down.

I explain that the group who chose to take the risks will do most of the action but make it clear to the other group that their awareness of their reaction to what is happening is vital.

The group is told that we are going to play with the concept of being different. The word 'play' is used because it is always easier to under-stand a different perspective or to approach a new idea if it is in the form of creative play. Those with the material are going to sculpt the other person into a 'deformed' shape. They may wish to give the person a hump or huge stomach. They may choose to turn the arms into stumps but whatever they sculpt has to look grotesque. Students may decide to stuff cotton balls in their mouths. This helps create a further challenge in a vocal exercise used later. Music from a concerto for violin strings and organ from Bach's *La Stravaganza, Op. 4 Concerto No. 5* is played in order that the sculpting begins in an atmosphere of rejoicing.

EXERCISE ONE

The deformed characters are to move lightly around the room to the music. [Side One from *Visions of Paradise* by Japetus is appropriate.] They are to imagine they are walking in space. The other group is going to sit at one end of the room observing like an audience at a play. Then the deformed group are told to move lightly to the back of the room and huddle in a group. I take one of the tennis balls and throw it. I want the impact of the ball to shock rather than hurt. Naturally, the deformed group, feeling under attack, will huddle closer together. I encourage this reaction. When the last ball has been thrown (by me) they are told to freeze together and listen to the next instructions. Note: I always throw the balls. Insensitive students could hurt and/or destroy the atmosphere.

Experiencing empathy for the outsider

EXERCISE TWO

The music is repeated. A slower passage has been chosen for this exercise. Each time I bang my pole on the ground, one of the deformed is to slowly look up and only when they are looking at the audience fully, will they suddenly allow their face to break into a shy but mischievous smile. They are numbered off so they know the order in which they will look up. They are told the particular quality of the smile they are to give (shy and mischievous).

Self acceptance

EXERCISE THREE

Each person in the group is to come forward, one at a time and sing a nursery rhyme or any sweet song they know, trying their very best to do it well. They must use gesture and engage their audience as best they can. Their aim is to move the audience and their struggle is to overcome the audience not wishing to take them seriously. As this is a very difficult aim, I speak to the deformed group before they begin and tell them that on no account must they join in with any laughter.

Experiencing being Different

...becoming the invisible people

THE CIRCLE   As this lesson is very confronting for both groups we end the lesson by coming into the circle and discussing our reactions to each stage. If there is time the whole group will be given a choice between writing down their experience or drawing a picture. The group who weren't deformed are asked to choose between the extracts from Shakespeare or the poems and to take the material home and prepare it for the following week.

If the two lessons are concurrent, the half of the class who were the observers now prepare to become 'deformed'. They will read the selected literature and choose their speech or poem, while those who enacted the deformed persons gather fabrics and props and reflect on how they will dress the other group.

...becoming the invisible people

Lesson Fifteen

A word about use of resource material. As our school believes in the principle of ungraded classes, everyone studies similar texts. Students who have difficulty receive more help from both the teacher of that class and the school's resource teacher. We believe that the ideas and themes of the more complex texts such as Shakespeare should be available to everyone. Therefore the Shakespeare text under current study can be used. The class as part of their English language study will be acting out particular scenes. Even a student who doesn't know a speech, will certainly be familiar with it. There will be other students who, as part of a school or class production, will know all the speeches of the character they are portraying. Every student is playing with a set of obstacles which they choose to impose. As has already been suggested, coherence is secondary to intention. Many students choose to be unintelligible (as has already been suggested, some students put cotton balls in their mouths to make articulation difficult) as part of their characterisation. A student may prefer an easier vehicle for expression and, regardless of reading levels etc, choose a nursery rhyme or a song.

In the following lesson the groups change over so that the audience is now made up of the previous actors. The same lesson plan is followed but this time when they are doing the first exercise (that of moving around the room) music from *Visions of Paradise*, Japetus, First Vision, Side Two is used. I have found this music helps to bring in another perspective. The atmospheric difference in the two pieces of music is as follows. The first piece (Side One, used in Lesson Fourteen) is lyrical. The music in *this* lesson is chosen because it is more subtly evocative. As drama teachers we have to experiment with music because the choice in the end is highly individual. The response to the first group of deformed ones is often one of hilarity. The class could totally break up. This may go on for the entire performance of the first group and I allow this to happen. It is, generally speaking, an honest group reaction to seeing one's friends look so absurd.

When I play music evoking a more mysterious, even grave mood in this lesson, it allows the students a very different experience as they witness the absurd efforts of their friends. When the group is doing the exercise *(Exercise Two)* where they raise their faces one by one I also use this music. Finally, students may wish to speak of how they felt at different points. It is good to encourage such honest expression of feeling. If only *one* student understands the difficulty of expressing themselves poignantly when they look and feel unacceptable, it is enough.

Part Two

Drama
and the Teaching
of Novels

Drama and the Teaching of Novels

On the following pages are some of the exercises I do in conjunction with the study of novels.

Unless the ideas of a novel or play are acted out by the students the experience is in danger of remaining academic. It is certainly true for me that all worthwhile experiences of fiction offer a glimpse into the writer's world picture and it is within the confines of this picture, that the chosen characters live and feel. So the more we can live out their experience the more we will understand the world picture which contains them.

'LORD OF THE FLIES'

The difference between comedy and tragedy

The first element which strikes me about *Lord of the Flies* is its dramatic tension. This novel presents a wonderful opportunity to witness how tension works and something about the differences between comedy and tragedy. The difference between comic tension and dramatic tension is quite subtle and often too difficult for students to grasp. The question becomes even more complicated when we try to discover the different elements which distinguish comedy from tragedy.

If we examine the television series *Fawlty Towers*, which was highly successful in terms of its comic script, and ask ourselves what still makes it so funny, we immediately focus on the character Basil Fawlty. One of the first things we notice is that Basil (like Malvolio in *Twelfth Night*) doesn't know he is funny. In trying to do his best he creates situation after situation of comic tension and he never really understands why it all goes wrong.

What then is the difference between the comic tension in *Fawlty Towers* and the dramatic tension in *Lord of the Flies*?

The tragic hero/heroine can never escape self knowledge. Ralph in *Lord of the Flies* increasingly understands the truth of his situation and we, the reader, fear for him because we can't see how he can escape death.

It has been suggested that in tragedy the hero's suffering leads to his/ her eventual death but that in comedy the comic hero (heroine), though battered and bruised, survives. We know for certain that in *Lord of the Flies* Ralph would never have survived without the intervention of adults.

In the drama exercises which follow one of the main aims will be to assist the students to have a better understanding of the function of dramatic tension.

In this series of exercises we will establish the following:

a) Difference between comic tension and dramatic tension.

b) The importance of conflicting objectives in dramatic tension.

c) The need for a powerful adversary in the development of conflict.

INTRODUCTION

I discuss with the class their perceived differences between the forms of comedy and tragedy but deliberately leave out discussion of the genres of farce and melodrama at this stage because neither seeks to engage the audience emotionally.

We discuss our experiences of live drama, film and television. In this discussion we concentrate on their feeling reaction. Why did a particular film or play make them laugh or cry? I ask them to concentrate on a character who has made them laugh and to picture what quality in this character gave rise to this feeling. They are then asked to think of a character whose situation aroused feelings of pity and sadness and to discover what it was about this character which made them convincing in this role.

I concentrate on aspects of movement and body language as well as facial expression, bringing their attention to the way silence and stillness are frequently used to express feelings of expectation and fear. We then examine the question of how the feeling of expectation can be funny; or alternatively, if it isn't actually frightening, at least unsettling.

Importance of audience identification with character

EXERCISE ONE

I ask them to write down their memories of their first day at school. After this is completed some students are asked to share this experience with everyone. They are then required to write down any memory of an awkward mishap which occurred at sometime in their life due to nervousness. Again we share some of these experiences and then I ask them to picture how this event may have appeared to an onlooker who was totally uninvolved. We will probably reach a general concensus that it could, in that circumstance, appear very funny and that in order to move away from the comic aspect of the event, it would be necessary for the onlooker to feel some sympathy towards the character in the action.

I then ask them to picture someone they really admire. This may take a few minutes. It is important to stress the difference between admiration and adoration. They can choose someone they have never met.

I ask them to write down the qualities which they admire. Through reading out these qualities we all have the opportunity to deepen our understanding of the idea of "nobility of character". This then lays the groundwork for our examination of the characters of Ralph and Piggy.

Role of character in building dramatic tension

EXERCISE TWO

The students are asked to consider the simple action of walking into the room. Several students take it in turns to come into the room and present the following emotions in turn.

1. Tension — which has a dramatic base
2. Tension — which has a comic base

I suggest the importance of approaching the situation without too much reflection and see what happens. We then discuss which was the most difficult of the two emotions and why this was so.

The aim here is, that we will discover, without knowing anything about the character, it is harder to build dramatic tension than comic tension.

EXERCISE THREE   *Extension of character work from Exercise Two*
The class is divided into pairs and each pair is asked to improvise a mimed scene which will be presented in two different ways—i.e. one version will be comic, the other will be dramatic. They choose a very simple scene which is to consist of an entrance, an exchange and an exit by one of the characters. I ask them to be sure they establish the mood of the scene and the place in which it occurs. In the dramatic scene, they are to imagine that the protagonist has some of the admirable qualities described previously. In the comic scene I ask that the protagonist be played as a fool. They have three minutes to organise both scenes. We present these scenes to each other. In response to the different perform-ances, the class will be able to distinguish between their different reactions. Part of the purpose of this exercise is to see if their reactions to a 'dramatic' performance made them laugh rather than feel sympathy.

We will then differentiate between drama, melodrama and farce. It will be pointed out that in both melodrama and farce there will be no emotional involvement of the audience. We also look at our different reactions to a dramatic piece of live theatre or film and a successful comic scene. We may come up with the fact that there is a *greater iden-tification* with the character in the dramatic scene. Basil Fawlty makes us laugh but we do not admire or deeply sympathise with his predicaments. I will then play a short sequence from *The Gold Rush*, starring Charlie Chaplin, in which we will witness the narrowing of this difference in terms of identification and the resulting narrowing of the difference between comedy and tragedy.

EXERCISE FOUR   *Character and motivation of Ralph and Piggy*
I read the section from the novel which describes the first meeting of Ralph and Piggy.

I ask the class to write a brief description of both boys based upon each person's individual response to this meeting. The aim here is to discover the differences between the two boys before we move onto the next part of this exercise. I also ask them to write down both boys' motivations. What do they each want? I point out that it's likely that their objectives are different.

The class is then asked to write down which of the boys is more powerful in this scene and to give a reason for this opinion.

NOTE: Instead of the class writing I may choose these issues as a basis for class discussion.

Finally they write about the tension in this scene.

The class is divided into pairs and each pair is asked to re-enact the scene showing:

> **character**
> **motivation**
> **the power relations between the boys**
> **tension**

I allow about five minutes for the groups to make their decision about how they will re-enact the scene and then we watch different pairs performing.

We form a circle and discuss what has emerged from the improvisations. One important issue here will be the degree of the reader's identification with each boy.

The role of the powerful adversary in the creation of dramatic tension

In the chapter "Huts on the Beach" we experience the wide gap between the objectives of Ralph and Jack which increases the tension between them.

EXERCISE FIVE

"They've put on green branches", muttered Ralph. "I wonder!" He screwed up his eyes and swung round to search the horizon.
"Got it!"
Jack shouted so loudly that Ralph jumped.
"What? Where? Is it a ship?"
But Jack was pointing to the high declivities that led down from the mountain to the flatter part of the island.
"Of course! They'll lie up there— they must do, when the sun's too hot—"
Ralph gazed bewildered at his rapt face.
" — they get up high. High up and in the shade, resting during the heat, like cows at home— "
"I thought you saw a ship!"
"We could steal up on one—paint our faces so they wouldn't see— perhaps surround them and then ——"
Indignation took away Ralph's control.
"I was talking about smoke! Don't you want to be rescued? All you can talk about is pig, pig, pig!"

I ask the class what it is which makes this scene so tense. We will discuss the two characters involved, their individual strengths and weaknesses. I want the class to understand the need for a powerful adversary, one who really challenges the hero, in a conflict. They are then asked to think of the people who challenge them most in their own life and thus confirm that this is also the case in their personal reality.

We will then consider the opening scene of the novel and compare the tension in that scene with the one under discussion.

EXERCISE SIX   *Importance of each character's objectives.*

We examine a scene from *Painted Faces and Long Hair* which shows clearly the next stage in the development of the conflict between these two characters. We have looked at the importance of strength. Now we consider in more detail the way in which tension arises from different objectives.

He spread his arms wide.
"You should have seen the blood!"
The hunters were more silent now, but at this they buzzed again. Ralph flung back his hair. One arm pointed at the empty horizon. His voice was loud and savage, and struck them into silence.
"There was a ship."
Jack, faced at once with too many awful implications, ducked away from them. He laid a hand on the pig and drew his knife. Ralph brought his arm down, fist clenched, and his voice shook.
"There was a ship. Out there. You said you'd keep the fire going and you let it out!"

In this scene we witness the outcome of the clash between their different objectives. Ralph's objective has just failed because he didn't get the necessary support. Jack's jubilation is smashed by his recognition that on some level he is seen as a failure.

The class is divided into groups and each group enacts two scenes of their own design. The first scene should express conflicting interests between two powerful characters. The second scene should express the outcome when both of the characters' interests are defeated through lack of support.

'A WIZARD OF   The key to this text is the presence of magic and supernatural powers.
EARTHSEA'   Underlying this world of magic is, however, a story of self-discovery. A theme which is made accessible to children through the excitement of wizards and witches who create mystery and enchantment. We have witnessed this device in such movies as *Star Wars* and *E.T.* where the mystery of space replaces the world of wizard and witches. These movies also express the idea that personal challenge is essential to the growth of the individual.

When studying a text like *A Wizard of Earthsea* I find it is a good idea to show one of these types of film as they help to clarify the themes I'm exploring with the class. Challenge is not only something to overcome, it makes life exciting. One can choose whether to see difficulties in one's life as just another hassle or as one's own story of adventure. It seems to me that what Ursula Le Guin is saying is that to confront the shadows in ourselves can be an exciting adventure.

When we study novels, we generally talk a lot about plot, character and theme. Sometimes a novel calls our attention to one of these aspects and we may notice that this aspect appears to be the central key to coming to grips with the novel. To me the key to understanding *A Wizard of Earthsea* is the study of the theme. Theme is however a fairly subtle concept for a twelve year old and so my first endeavour would be to differentiate between theme and plot.

Lesson Thirteen also contains exercises relating to witches and wizards.

Plot

I ask the class to form a circle. I then divide the group into a series of partners A and B. Assuming the size of the group is eighteen, the first nine, for example, all those students sitting on my left will be A and the others in the circle will all be B. A will work with B who is sitting more or less opposite on the other side of the circle. Students A are then asked to take it in turns to begin a story—a few sentences are enough—which their partner will continue when it is their turn. After each A has begun the story, each B will continue for a few sentences. Because of the position of partners A and B in the circle [opposite each other], there will be a delay before each story continues. This means that students B must listen very carefully in order to hold the information until it is his/her turn. The limitation on the Bs is that they must logically continue the story.

Obviously the quality of the story unfolding will very much depend on the group's previous experience in story telling and the individual children's creative ability. My aim, however, is not to elicit fabulous stories (although this is nice if it happens) but to allow the class to experience the creation of a plot without any intention to consciously develop a theme. The story will therefore unfold without any prior discussion as to intention.

EXERCISE ONE

Theme

I choose a fairly simple story which is easy to read but which has a very strong theme and I read it aloud to the class. One of my personal favourites for this exercise is *The Velveteen Rabbit* by Margery Williams. This not only has a strong theme, it also evokes childhood memories about our favourite toys and, therefore, in most of us who read it, or preferably, listen to it being read, evokes a memory associated with strong feelings. And it is this kind of experience which can lead to a real understanding of issues which lie beyond the plot. The plot of *The Velveteen Rabbit* is essentially to do with a stuffed toy rabbit who becomes real. But of central interest to the story is the theme of what it means to be "real".

"What is REAL?" asked the Rabbit one day, when they were lying side by side near the nursery fender, before Nana came to tidy the room. "Does it mean having things that buzz inside you and a stick-out handle?"

"Real isn't how you are made", said the Skin Horse. "It's a thing that happens to you. When a child loves you for a long, long time, not just to play with, but Really loves you, then you become Real."

"Does it hurt?" asked the Rabbit.

"Sometimes," said the Skin Horse, for he was always truthful. "When you are Real, you don't mind being hurt."

"Does it happen all at once, like being wound up," he asked, "or bit by bit?"

"It doesn't happen all at once," said the Skin Horse. "You become. It

EXERCISE TWO

takes a long time. That's why it doesn't often happen to people who break easily, or have sharp edges, or who have to be carefully kept. Generally, by the time you are Real, most of your hair has been loved off, and your eyes drop out and you get loose in the joints and very shabby. But these things don't matter at all, because once you are Real you can't be ugly, except to people who don't understand."

After I have read this story to the class we talk about the memories and emotions it has raised. I have read this story or heard it being read to all age groups and although it invariably begins with memories of childhood and toys which were particularly well loved, it always seems to raise questions about the difference between people who are phoney and people who are REAL.

After this discussion, I ask the class for some of the differences between this kind of story and the stories which developed in the circle between the pairs. This provides them with an opportunity to distinguish between telling a series of events in story form and telling a story with an underlying theme.

EXERCISE THREE   **Mime based on a theme**

The class is asked to run around the room in a circle very fast without touching anyone and when they hear the drum beat everyone will stop still until they hear the word "relax". I want to introduce disciplined movement before beginning the main part of the lesson. I then tell them to run and every time they hear a drum beat they are to freeze. A new movement using any of the following is then called out:

jumping	turning
skipping	taking giant steps
hopping	crow walking

They are then told that the drum will now give them the directions. I go through the various movement possibilities above in that order and tell them the drum will indicate which movement by the number of drum beats; one beat indicates running, two beats indicate jumping and so on.

We do this exercise for a few minutes and then everyone is asked to lie on the floor, make themselves comfortable and be very still. They are to allow their bodies to develop a shape which best describes the ideas I give them verbally. They are to keep their eyes closed throughout this exercise. Each of the following words is said slowly and I give the group time to slowly take on a shape which explores the movement possibilities of the idea associated with the word.

greed	deceit	shyness
cunning	unhappiness	curiosity
dominance	sadness	joy

They are then asked to choose one of the previously listed words. When they have chosen a word, they will develop the idea further, without looking at anyone else or moving away from their own area. They do this for a short while (a minute or so) and then I ask them to freeze and hold a shape which best expresses the idea associated with the word.

Mime on the theme of greed. **EXERCISE FOUR**
The word greed: the basis for the next exercise.

In this exercise we will use mostly movement to convey the meaning but each group is allowed to use a little gobbledegook to assist in getting the meaning across. I tell them their play is going to be on the theme of greed and there will be a basic plot. The plot is as follows:

> There are two people walking along the road. Suddenly one of them sees a very unusual pair of shoes lying on the ground. Both people want to try them on. The stronger of the two wins. Once the shoes are on the character, they find they can fly and begin to tease the other character with this new found skill. Many embellishments of style in flying may be added. At length the character tires and lies down to sleep still wearing the shoes. The other character now sees an opportunity to try them on. However, the task is difficult since the character wearing the shoes could wake up with the slightest disturbance.

The class is asked to improvise on this basic plot and develop the two characters; the strong one being able to grab what they desire, while the weaker one must develop cunning in order to obtain the shoes.

I have deliberately chosen a negative personality trait because it leads more directly to the theme of *A Wizard of Earthsea*.

Most of the stories we read relate in some way to our mythological roots and it is to one of these myths that I would normally turn at this stage. Two people who have influenced my approach to drama, Dorothy Heathcote and Peter Brook both, in their work, reflect the importance of myth, fairytale and legend in the creative life of us all.

One can of course look at novels as an academic exercise. But if we are truly interested in the psychological health of the child we can go a step further to help them to see the connection between the adventure in the novel and how it relates to them in their lives. It is not the role of literature to establish some clearly defined set of rules to guide behaviour but a chance for the child to experience in story form the challenges they one day will confront in one form or another.

The celebrated myth of Ariadne and Theseus, the hero slayer of the Minotaur is also a story about the greed of King Minos. King Minos hired the celebrated artist craftsman Daedalus to invent and construct for him a labyrinth, in which to hide something of which the palace was ashamed. There was a monster on the premises which had been born to Pasiphae, the wife of Minos, after she had been seduced by a magnificent snow-white, sea-born bull. The bull in question had been sent by the god Poseidon, long ago, when Minos was contending with his brothers for the throne. Minos had asserted that the throne was his, by divine right, and had prayed to the sea god to send up the bull out of the ocean, as a sign. He had sealed the prayer with a vow to sacrifice the bull immediately as an offering. The bull appeared and Minos took the throne; but when he beheld the majesty of the beast, he decided to keep it and to substitute another bull as the sacrifice. Thus the primary fault of what happened was the king's greed.

After telling this story, I then turn to the novel and in particular to the chapter titled *The Loosing of the Shadow*. We read the section which preceeds that event.

"Now," Ged said to Jasper, quietly as before, "what are you going to do to prove yourself my superior, Jasper?"

"I don't have to do anything, Goatherd. Yet I will. I will give you a chance ... an opportunity. Envy eats you like a worm in an apple. The shapeless mass of darkness he had lifted split apart. It sundered, and a pale spindle of light gleamed between his opened arms, a faint oval reaching from the ground up to the height of his raised hands."

In seeking to compete with Jasper, envy being the prime motivating force, Ged has loosed the shadow which will pursue him through the ensuing pages of the novel.

After reading this section I ask the class to move the chairs and tables to the back of the room in preparation for the next exercise.

EXERCISE FIVE The class is asked to disperse throughout the room and find a spot where they feel they will not be distracted. They then lie down and close their eyes while I conduct a short relaxation. At the conclusion of the relaxation, I ask them to slowly stretch and stand up so that their knees are bent. They are told that they can now open their eyes and begin moving around the room, their knees still bent. As they move they are to chant the following: "so what!". When this has been said (preferably growled) a few times, I ask them to continue moving but every time they meet someone they are to take it in turns to say "who do you think you are?"

EXERCISE SIX Everyone lies on the floor. They make themselves as small as possible and imagine they are mice, investigating very timidly, their immediate environment. This is done without any student relating to other members of the class. It is important that they maintain constant action. I tell them to be watchful, alert and constantly investigating. They then freeze in order to feel the smallness of the animal. They next take on the form of a cat increasing the power of their movements as they explore their immediate environment. I ask them to freeze in a powerful position and to feel the sensation of that power.

EXERCISE SEVEN This exercise involves playing with the idea of boasting. I ask the class to stand as tall as they can and to begin strutting around the room shouting out at each person they meet how fantastic they are at everything they do. This will be very noisy but it is essential that everyone does it together with no-one listening to anyone in particular. It functions as an icebreaker for the next exercise.

EXERCISE EIGHT The class divide into pairs and sit on the floor opposite their partner. I always stipulate the maximum distance apart they are to be. In order to work together the partners need to be in close contact and so I check if any pair is further than a few centimetres apart and tell them to sit closer. Beside each person there is drawing paper and crayons. They are asked to close their eyes and picture some of their positive qualities or pleasant points and then to picture their difficult points or negative aspects. They then take it in turn to tell each other both aspects.

Each person is asked to draw their shadow. We discuss the fact that the shadow which Ged is facing is like a meeting between the different parts of oneself. I suggest to the class that it is a good idea not to judge that part of oneself which creates the kind of difficulty which is explored in an extreme way in *A Wizard of Earthsea*. Their drawings do not need to take a form as clearly defined as the shadow in the novel. It may well be a vague and misty drawing. I suggest that the important part to capture is its colour. Music by Phillip Glass which was the soundtrack for the film *The Thin Blue Line* is played. I choose it because it is likely to be less familiar and because it has a dramatic quality which suits the theme of the novel which we are exploring.

Some teachers may question the wisdom of such a personal exploration and I acknowledge that great care should be taken before embracing this kind of exercise. Precautions taken involve the following:

1. Respect for each student's perception of their own shadow. The teacher should never attempt an interpretation of the student's visual expression. I am offering an experience which can deepen the understanding of issues in the novel. As I am not a psychologist I do not talk at all about their work. They will draw and I provide a musical context for the event.

2. The teacher should know the group of students very well and feel their trust.

3. The exercise must never be rushed and there must be enough time at the end for discussion.

THE CIRCLE

At least ten minutes before the end of the lesson, I ask the class to divide once again into the pairs they were in before. In this time they can talk to each other about any aspect of the lesson or their drawing if they so wish.

Finally, they're asked to close their eyes for a couple of minutes. Meanwhile, I give a very brief relaxation session before asking them to picture themselves as they might look when they feel really good. This is so that the final image they take from the lesson is positive.

Part Three

The School
Production

The School Production

The school production is for many teachers and parents "the thing that has to be done each year". We have all (I hope, sympathetically) heard the cry from the English department, "What are we going to do this year?", a question which has again emerged for us at Korowal School.

At the moment I am working with a very small group of committed students who meet me outside school hours. Each producer has their own limitations and restrictions which are peculiar to their own school and situation.

LIMITATIONS AND RESTRICTIONS

1. We are a small school numbering about eighty in the high school. This means that if we put on a large production, such as *A Midsummer Night's Dream* (which we produced last year) I will have to work with some students who will find the learning of lines extremely difficult. One of the leading roles in last year's play was undertaken by a student whose success in normal school testing was very low. The play for this student was a time of personal achievement.

2. Being situated at Leura in the Blue Mountains, where travel is extremely difficult, rehearsal time is restricted and has to be organised according to limited transport facilities.

3. We do not have a school hall in which to rehearse and can generally count on no more than five rehearsals in the hall in which the play will be performed. This means that lighting and dress rehearsal time are limited.

4. A very small budget (about $1200) and $900 of this will be payment for the hall.

On the positive side, although our resources are limited, we have professional help free of charge in the areas of costume design, set design and lighting from the school parent population, which make an enormous contribution to the overall presentation.

AIMS

Given the above, my aims are as follows:
1. To produce a play which aims at excellence.
2. To provide a valuable learning experience for the students involved. This will hopefully encompass the following:
a) Co-operating with others in a group.
b) Commitment to a group project.
c) Learning stage skills and applying known drama skills to present a polished performance.

d) Enjoyment

e) Development of practical knowledge in the technical aspects of theatre.

f) Exhilaration and satisfaction which comes from working hard to achieve personal excellence.

g) Greater self confidence and encouragement of independence of spirit.

h) Develop individual creativity.

Given the above aims, I find myself in the unenviable position of discarding a play I have been working on for at least two months. After this period of two hour rehearsals each week after school, one might well say that little has been achieved as the result of this effort. How did it happen?

For at least three weeks before rehearsals began on this particular play, the group who have studied drama with me for four years, workshopped various plays. We decided on this play and started rehearsals. As time went by some of the group approached me and suggested that most were less than happy with the play. They felt it was too sophisticated for their age group and gave them too little scope in acting skills and interpretation. We sat down and discussed the implications. It would mean workshopping other plays which would take up valuable time and, as time was already lost, this would put us all under considerable pressure. On reflection, I felt their criticisms were legitimate and so we have begun researching other plays.

Leaving this current problem aside for the moment, I would like to now go back to last year's production of *A Midsummer Night's Dream*.

There are three main stages to preparation of a play.

1. Familiarisation. This is achieved through the following:

a) Improvisation

b) Rehearsal of different scenes

c) Learning of lines

With Shakespeare's play I wanted the students to develop slowly into their characters without any preconceptions as to how that part should or could be played. For some students however this did not evolve until a few weeks before production.

2. Understanding the rhythms of the play.

In this play understanding the rhythms is vital as it is an interplay between the world of ordinary mortals and the world of magical beings. It gets more complicated too, because the world of ordinary beings is further divided into two layers of society's fabric: the aristocracy and the more ordinary world of the working people. These three worlds merge and move apart as one does in a dance. To capture this quality is, I believe, the secret. One can never develop such subtleties until the students know their lines but once this is achieved specific movement direction which takes into account such rhythms is possible. I don't think being dogmatic about where students move on the stage induces anything apart from rigidity. If one of the aims is to assist individual creativity it can best be served by encouraging looseness and independence of spirit.

In *A Midsummer Night's Dream* we worked with exploration of three different types of movement patterns:

a) Light, quick movements for the fairy world.
This called for emphasis on the top part of the body.
b) Slower, more regal movements for the aristocracy where movement is centred around the hips.
c) Slower movement for the working people, centred around the buttocks, thighs and knees.

At this stage of production, which would be at least two months into rehearsals, students will have begun making their costumes under the guidance of some of the parents and teachers.

3. Integration

I have now grown used to the fact that over the last four weeks of rehearsals, students frequently come up to me and say "I've just begun to understand my part". Of central importance at this stage, is The Drama Camp. This can vary in length from a weekend to a week.

For *A Midsummer Night's Dream* the camp lasted a week and it was invaluable.

This time of integration is a period of intense work. We video our rehearsals as much as possible and at the end of each rehearsal sit down and watch it together discussing strengths and weaknesses. Tensions run high at this stage. In larger schools it may be that everyone in the cast is an "old trooper" but at Korowal, as has already been suggested, very inexperienced actors and actresses will be working alongside students who have studied drama with me for up to five years. This can create tension between the two groups and in terms of cast cohesion it therefore becomes an important time. They can either support each other or view the whole as an event of separate people putting in individual performances. One of the symptoms of such tension is that students in minor parts may begin grumbling about time taken for rehearsals. There may also be resentment towards the so-called "stars". None of this would be apparent if I was totally authoritarian in manner. Everyone would be too frightened to say anything. This could appear to be an advantage but individual antagonism whether stated or suppressed would affect the final outcome.

One of the most important ways one can develop cast co-operation (which is always there to a smaller or larger extent) is to have a group discussion at the end of each rehearsal.

At this stage I begin to give very close direction, refining and making the movements of some characters more specific while in others there may be the need for a greater largesse of character and movement. Everyone then has the chance to view the changes on video.

In every school there are students in the cast who are going to become sick at the last minute. This is always a challenge for any director. In *A Midsummer Night's Dream* Puck did not turn up to the dress rehearsal (there were only two such rehearsals) and her mother phoned me to say that her child had a severe asthma attack and it was even possible she may not be able to perform on the night. What to do? Obviously the part was an important one. The effect of this news on the rest of the cast was devastating. Students were wondering if their pursuit of excellence was worthwhile. Amongst the players was a student so keen that she knew nearly all of the lines of the other characters. She also happened to be an exceptionally good actress whose chief virtue was that she did not display "star" characteristics. By this I mean she rarely grumbled, was always on time and was attentive not only to her own part but to the action of the whole so that she always knew what was happening, never missed a cue and knew her lines by the end of the first few weeks. What a treasure, a boon in the life of any teacher/director. This student happened to be playing the role of Hermia. The whole of that dress rehearsal became a salvage operation of the play with Hermia playing her own part as well as the part of Puck. Well might anyone ask how this could happen since there were two extremely sticky situations of costume change and one required Hermia to be on the stage asleep along with Puck. We decided to get Hermia to lie behind a stage block (the bed of Titania and the throne in the final scenes) so she could sneak off stage while pretending to be asleep. It was going to be awkward but we all realised it could be done. It was also interesting for the cast to witness a different style Puck whose performance was exceptional given the circumstances. But the most important result was that everyone knew the play could be salvaged.

CASTING FOR *"A MIDSUMMER NIGHT'S DREAM"*

It's a good idea to allow those wishing to participate in the school production to familiarise themselves with the parts available before casting. To achieve this, copies of the play are made available and can be passed around amongst those interested a couple of weeks before casting. Everyone is then told to meet after school on a particular day. When all the interested students are assembled on that afternoon I begin by telling them of their obligations should they accept a part. I particularly warn those in the group who I know are enthusiasts of many extra-curricular activities that over the final weeks there will probably be weekend rehearsals and they must be certain they can fulfil their obligations to the group before accepting a part. We discuss the plot of the play and the different characters involved before students read parts.

While they read it is important to not only listen to their voice, but watch their movement and their physical suitability for the part. Physical suitability not only implies weight, height and personal features but the energy a person has. A student may have a quickness about their movement which will be particularly suitable for the role of Oberon for example. The character Oberon demands a light energy in terms of movement and in the casting I already had my eye on one student who combined this lightness of movement with talent and experience. Where possible one should take into account work done previously. Students who have already demonstrated reliability and commitment as well as ability to absorb direction are going to offer the play stability. I will also be looking to make sure an inexperienced actor/actress will have an experienced actor/actress working in the same scene. This means that the inexperienced player can gain confidence from the knowledge that if they need help it will probably be there.

If one takes the time to really look at the students you can actually see the different characters emerging. It is a good idea not to give out the parts before allowing the characters to distil in one's mind for a while. With *A Midsummer Night's Dream* Oberon was the first to become clear, partly because of the lightness of his movements but also because he is a sensitive boy who can more easily get in touch with the child inside who understands the world of magic. Puck was also chosen largely on the basis of her movement and personality. She is sensitive and has a strong sense of mischief, qualities important for the role. She is small, in contrast to Oberon who is tall, but like him has a lightness in her movements. Sometimes in the less major roles, characters will be chosen for different reasons. The fairies were mostly at an ungainly age. By that I mean girls who were very self-conscious on stage and whose movements reflected this. The play offered them the chance to gain more self-confidence in nature and bearing.

FAMILIARISATION AND IMPROVISATION

We began preparation for the play by improvising comic themes. In Lesson Four we explored mime and clowning and I would begin this introductory period with very similar exercises.

EXERCISE ONE

Two people sit opposite one another. They are to look into each other's eyes. They commence this when I tell them and they continue for about two minutes. This is, of course, embarrassing and, although ostensibly simple, is in fact quite difficult. It is also a very quick ice breaker as it demands a lifting of barriers which will be essential if the group is to work unselfconsciously with one another. I then ask them to each find someone else to sit opposite, someone they would not automatically gravitate towards.

We repeat this process several times so that students can familiarise themselves with each other.

EXERCISE TWO

Each student finds a partner and sits opposite. They will take it in turns to tell each other about their lives, where they were born and where they first went to school, what their interests are and what they enjoy doing best. Then each pair will take it in turns to introduce their partner to the rest of the group. This introduction however will be a great exaggeration of what each has just heard and the aim will be to boast about the person they are introducing. Students enjoy the fun of this and it prepares the ground for the ensuing exercises which are to develop the comic element.

EXERCISE THREE

As indicated above, the clown exercises from Lesson Four of this book will be introduced. These exercises are to loosen students by introducing the element of play. They are also beginning to experience comic tension as conflict develops between the two clowns. I further develop the idea of comic tension through the following exercises:

1. Each student is to mime washing a floor. They will each take a mop and bucket and simply wash an imaginary floor. When I am satisfied that they are quite focussed on this exercise the following complications will be introduced.

Imaginary people are crossing the floor. At first it is easier to imagine just one—the antagonist. The antagonist walks across the floor and just when the floorwasher has repaired the damage, walks across again. The student is required to develop this simple scene in their own time. If this is going well I may increase the number of imaginary people crossing the floor.

2. Everyone chooses a partner. Each pair is to decide who is the waiter and who the difficult customer. They are to develop a mime scenario around the idea of a clumsy waiter trying unsuccessfully to satisfy the needs of a fastidious customer.

EXERCISE FOUR

Another element in the play *A Midsummer Night's Dream* is the experience of exclusion. To understand this better I ask the students to form groups of three. On the floor I draw with chalk a triangle for each group and each member of the trio is to stand on one of the points of the triangle. Two of the students are to turn towards each other and take it in turns to tell about a good time they had recently. The third member of the group must stand perfectly still and without comment listen to the other two talk. They then each swap positions so that each has a turn to experience being the one excluded. As they swap around they will be given another topic to talk about, e.g. a funny film they have seen recently, a difficulty or good time they recently experienced with a teacher, parent or friend. At the conclusion of this exercise we form a circle and talk about what we experienced.

EXERCISE FIVE

A most important element in the play is that of magic. As teenagers, the group as a whole will be pretty much removed from this and it can be quite difficult to evoke. The world of childhood magic is for most becoming remote as their interest grows in their awakening adulthood.

I have elaborated on relevant exercises in the section of this book which deals with witches and wizards—Lesson Thirteen.

EXERCISE SIX

As teenage love is an important theme in this play, we will watch the film of *Romeo and Juliet* by Zefferelli and discuss the difference in the feeling quality between these two Shakespearean plays. What I want them to feel is that in *A Midsummer Night's Dream* there is a strong feeling of playfulness which, though present in *Romeo and Juliet*, is overshadowed by the feeling of impending doom. In the play *A Midsummer Night's Dream* love may finally be seen as a state worthy of respect but throughout the confusions of the play it is also seen to be a state in which a lot of silliness can occur. To tap that silliness without becoming cynical about love is therefore an important aim. To develop this idea of silliness a little further I used the following exercise.

The students bring to the next rehearsal any items of evening dress they can forage from home and friends. The girls are to bring makeup and before the rehearsal begins they are to dress up in these borrowed items. I have prepared a tape containing such tunes as Marlene Dietrich singing *Falling in Love Again, Move Closer* sung by Phyllis Nelson, *Lady in Red* by Chris de Burgh. We dance to these songs and everyone takes a turn to dance with one another in a way which exaggerates the spirit of the song. Such play allows some objectivity, distance and fun to enter the mix.

REHEARSALS   Until students have learned their lines there is little one can do with movement and so I set realistic deadlines as to how soon the cast should know their lines. This will be no longer than two months. By this time the cast shouldn't need to hold their scripts and a prompt will be used. Until lines are learned we will concentrate on developing the character and helping the student to get a sense of mannerisms this character would have in both movement and expression. I will also draw their attention to the particular relationship between characters but most of all we will be looking at voice.

VOICE   By voice I mean diction, projection, meaning and character. One of the hardest problems is to get students to be heard in a large hall without amplification. However, though I am aware of the problem, at this stage we will only be looking for a level of audibility where they can be heard in the rehearsal room. This is because diction, meaning and character must be given priority. Once a student has developed a way of delivering lines, it is very hard to change, whereas projection can be developed at any stage. You can't give a student too many tasks at once.

MEANING   Students are quite adept at parroting passages, i.e. reading passages without any understanding at all. So the first issue is that of meaning. You have to check that they understand the passage both as a passage and within the context of the play as a whole.

CHARACTER   Once this is understood, only then can one move onto the interpretation of the passage in terms of the particular character. Although this involves cast discussions it is in the main an individual effort. This is a much more subtle task and requires that the student has really studied the part. If the student is not capable of doing this, and I have taught such students, the only way around this is for the director to sit down with the student and discuss the character and the meaning of the lines. One must be careful not to put anyone down for their inability in this area. It is not their fault and from my experience students doing a play generally give of their best.

REHEARSALS OF THE SCRIPT   When I start on a play and a reading has occurred, I concentrate on the first few scenes of the play. Only when these scenes are working in terms of understanding and character interpretation can the rest of the play be looked at. At first everyone is naturally quite excited. This generates much energy and makes the lot of the director easy. However, after two months of rehearsing one night each week enthusiasm begins to wane and a good director must be aware that students will need to be pushed through this next period. Otherwise absenteeism will occur and the play itself will lose momentum. I am always frank about this with the students and tell them in advance this will happen and make it quite clear that anyone not being consistent will be dropped. This is a very valuable time for the cast as the challenge is to persevere with an idea whose newness has disappeared.

UNDERSTANDING THE RHYTHMS OF THE PLAY

As has been suggested in an earlier section there are three different worlds in *A Midsummer Night's Dream* and the delight of this play is the way in which these three worlds interweave. Each world has its own conflict and eventual resolution which become mutually inter-dependent, giving the play its sense of completeness. The play seems to be saying that life without any of these three worlds would be incomplete. The physical world of Bottom and his friends has a vitality which the more refined world of Hermia and the lovers can not access. The poetic quality of the play on the other hand arises from the world of Puck, Oberon and Titania. However, the main focus of the dramatic conflict in the play is the confusing emotional situation of the young mortals with whom, we, the audience, can readily identify. The cast need to understand the different qualities present in each of these levels and the way they relate to different body movements.

It has been suggested that the physical movements of the fairy kingdom centres on the upper part of the body, the aristocratic world on the back and lower abdomen and for the ordinary mortals on the hips, knees and thighs. For the fairy world this implies a much lighter, more ethereal movement very close to the world of dance. The aristocratic world has a greater rigidity and the movement can reflect this by players keeping the back firm so that the body looks more controlled. In the world of the ordinary people, the centre of movement would be lower down as is suggested by the name Bottom. By playing with such movements the cast gets a sense of the essential differences between the three groups. I have also mentioned my reluctance to direct specific movements. Once you direct students too specifically their concern is centred on interpreting rather than becoming. To become a character is much harder but immeasurably more rewarding. Entrances and exits must of course direct them but they are encouraged to play with the directions given and not take them as the way it will finally be done.

The director should of course be watching the pattern of movements across the stage and make suggestions in terms of the scene as a whole rather like a painter organises the balance of ideas and colours for the canvas. This is fun and frequently members of the cast not on stage will sit with me and comment on the overall effect the scene has on them. At the end of a rehearsal we will often analyse what has happened and how it seems to be working. In this way the students become involved in the creative decision making.

INTEGRATION

The process of integration happens when the students understand how the characters interact in terms of the plot and themes and have knowledge of how the patterns of the play work in terms of movement. This never happens until the final weeks of rehearsal, in fact, often it is the last week.

The Drama Camp

*"One of the most
important ways to develop
cast co-operation is
to have a group discussion
at the end of each
rehearsal."*

Images taken from videotape

"Everyone would
be required to assess their
strengths and weaknesses..."

DRAMA CAMP   In *A Midsummer Night's Dream* I assisted this process by holding a drama camp. It is very valuable to take the cast of the school production somewhere where we can work without interruption. Generally it is somewhere close to the school, my home for instance but this time we raised money and went to a beautiful quiet spot where all our food was prepared, which meant we could concentrate entirely on the play for a week. The place we chose was in the Snowy Mountains. During this week we worked long hours and there was very little free time. The result was that everyone became very focussed on the play as there were no outside distractions. We took along a student whose sole object was to video each rehearsal session in which we were engaged. Below is an outline of our activities.

MORNING SESSION   We woke around 7 a.m. and after breakfast, which was at 8 a.m., we would either do the exercises outlined in Lesson One of this book for half an hour or go for a walk. If we chose the walk at some stage we would stop and do some of the stretching exercises in Lesson One. Immediately following this exercise we would commence rehearsal which would be videoed. We would run through the play and at the end sit in a circle and discuss our perceptions of the performance and the individual acting. Everyone would be required to assess themselves—strengths and weaknesses. This part of the session became increasingly important as time went by. If things went well we would take a break at about midday. If the rehearsal was sluggish some of the cast would bring morning tea to the rehearsal room where we would have a short break before the final run on any scene which looked weak. Lunch break was at 2 p.m.

AFTERNOON AND EVENING SESSIONS   We would recommence at about 3.30 p.m. and do another run through of the play which would finish around 6 p.m. when there would be a short break before dinner. If there was a scene which had really gone badly, that scene would be rehearsed in the evening after dinner. If an actor/actress had really missed cues during the day or badly fluffed their lines, they would be required to spend part of the evening going through the play with me or another member of the staff.

This was an incredibly heavy schedule for all of us and there were times when tempers were short. This was when the discussion time at the end of each rehearsal became very important. As well as discussing the play, grievances could be aired. One of the aims of the heavy schedule was to provide a challenge to students which normally only professional actors experience.

The end result was in fact a level of excellence which surprised parents and cast alike.

Since I began writing this section of the book we have in fact decided on our next play—*Romeo and Juliet*. As I only have about four boys to choose from for the male roles, some creative solutions are needed. My compensation is that two boys study fencing and enjoy mediaeval warfare which will be helpful. Oh well, you can't have everything!

Postscript

It should be said that this book was begun in 1988 and that the choice of *Romeo and Juliet* was made at the beginning of 1990.

Since that time, the play itself has been staged. This was an important event because for the students in the play, *Romeo and Juliet* represented their final theatrical work at Korowal. Having been the teacher of these students for five years, the play also represented the culmination of our shared drama experiences.

I am happy to say their work in the play reflected these years of application and commitment. We resolved the issue of a shortage of boys in the following way: the friar was played by a girl and some boys from a nearby school joined us to play the other male roles. For me it was a very exciting and fulfilling experience.

Final rehearsals...Romeo & Juliet